LLT, Liverpool's New Writing Theatre,
in association with Unity Theatre Liverpool
presents

The Doll Tower

by Ronan O'Donnell

Lowell Thomas & **MO**	Robin Sneller
Uxbridge	Paul Michael Stenton
Rude	Michael Ryan
Lawrence/Shaw	Garry Collins
Corporal Inglis	Stevie Hannan
Bruce	Graeme Rooney
Director	Graeme Maley
Designers	Angela Simpson
	and Graeme Maley
Lighting Designer	Phil Saunders
Composer	Brian Docherty
Production Manager	Jo Topping
Stage Manager	Jenny De Ornellas

First performed at Unity Theatre Liverpool
on Tuesday 27th September 2005

Garry Collins (*Lawrence/Shaw*)

Theatre includes *East Coast Chicken Supper* and *Mr Placebo* (Traverse Theatre); *Baby Doll, Handful of Dust, Cleo, Camping, Emmanuel and Dick, Snow White, Venice Preserved* and *The Queen of Spades* (Glasgow Citizens' Theatre); *Fierce, The Houghmagandie Pack* and *Decky Does a Bronco* (Grid Iron Theatre Company); *Dr Korczak's Example* (TAG Theatre Company); *Cave Dwellers* (7:84); *Beauty and the Beast, The Comedy of Errors, Cinderella* and *Romeo and Juliet* (Royal Lyceum Theatre, Edinburgh). Film includes *Dear Frankie* and *Count of Three*. TV includes *The Young Person's Guide to Becoming a Rock Star*, *Witch Craze* and *The Book Group*.

Stevie Hannan (*Corporal Inglis*)

Since graduating from RSAMD in 1988, Stevie has worked extensively throughout Scottish theatre, including productions for the Royal Lyceum, Wildcat Productions, Borderline, Cumbernauld and the Original Shakespeare Company among others. He has numerous TV appearances in *Taggart, Rebus, Doctor Finlay, The Real Tartan Army* and various TV commercials. He has appeared in at least a dozen short films and as Joe The Taxi in *Midnight Oil* and as Gus in *On a Clear Day*. This is Stevie's English stage debut and he is delighted to be working on such a great new piece of writing by O'Donnell.

Michael Ryan (*Rude*)

Theatre credits include *Hayfever* at Liverpool Playhouse; *The Trial* at Unity Theatre; *Dracula* at Everyman Theatre and *Pause for Thought* London's West End. TV includes Jimmy McGovern's *Dockers*, *In His Life* (NBC) and *Dream Team* (Sky One). Film includes *Revenger's Tragedy*.

Graeme Rooney (*Bruce*)

Graeme was born in Lanark. He trained at RSAMD where he graduated with a BA in Acting in 2004. He was selected by the school to perform in the William Poel Festival at the Globe and was also the 2004 Movement Award Winner. Since graduating he has played Puck in

Theatre Cryptics' *A Midsummer Night's Dream - the Opera*. He then went on to play the lead role in a short film for the BBC and could also be seen earlier in 2005 on TV in *Taggart* and an advert for British Gas.

Paul Michael Stenton (*Uxbridge*)

Paul served in the Royal Air Force for six years before he began training as an actor, graduating from the University of Salford. Paul's theatre credits include *Battle Statistic* and understudying in *Hobson's Choice* both at the Royal Exchange in Manchester. Past credits include Begbie in *Trainspotting* and Banquo in *Macbeth* for the Wide Boy Theatre Company; John Proctor in *The Crucible* for the Moving Parts Theatre Company and *Julius Caesar, More Light* and *Two* for Aspects Theatre Company. Paul's television credits include *Coronation Street, Bloody Murder I & II* (Granada), *Olaudah Equiano, Crimewatch UK* and *Real Story* (BBC).

Robin Sneller (*Lowell Thomas* and *MO*)

Theatre includes seasons at the Citizens' Theatre, Glasgow, the Edinburgh Royal Lyceum, Leicester Haymarket and Sheffield Crucible. In London his work includes *The Recruiting Officer, The Mountain Giants* and *The Wind in the Willows* at the National Theatre; *Damned for Despair* at the Gate Theatre; *Mind Millie for Me* for the Peter Hall Company; work for Unicorn Theatre and shows at the Lyric, Hammersmith and Soho Theatres. His one-man show, *Mayakovsky – a Tragedy* played in London, York, Sheffield and Edinburgh. Television includes *Rome, EastEnders, Holby City, The Bill* and *Wycliffe*.

Ronan O'Donnell (Writer)

Previous plays include *The Chic Nerds* (Traverse); *Spambam* (LookOut Theatre Company); *Brazil* (Theatre of Imagination); a version of Beijing author Wang Xiaoli's play *In the Bag* (Traverse); a version of *Lysistrata* and *The Ned's Lament* (Common Force Community Theatre). O'Donnell is currently working on a new commission for the Traverse Theatre Company. He lives in Edinburgh.

Graeme Maley (Director)

Director of LLT, Liverpool's New Writing Theatre. Assistant Director of the Traverse Theatre, Edinburgh, 1999-2000. Other theatre directing includes *The Body of a Woman* (Klink and Bang, Iceland); *Picasso's Women* (Assembly Rooms, Edinburgh Festival); *Macbeth* (Lemon Tree, Aberdeen); *The Danny Crowe Show* (Dundee Rep); *Brazil* (Latchmere Theatre, London and Arches, Glasgow); *Great Moments of Discovery* (Paines Plough); *The Ballad of James II* (The Scottish Playwrights' Studio).

Jo Topping (Production Manager)

Since moving to Liverpool three years ago, Jo has worked with Unity Theatre, Hope St LTD, Base Chorus, Spike Theatre, Rejects Revenge, Urban Straw, and the Everyman and Playhouse.

Phil Saunders (Lighting Designer)

Phil has worked extensively with dance and physical theatre companies in this country and abroad, most notably Sue MacLennan, Gregory Nash, The Cholmondeleys, Paula Hampson, Andrea Buckley and Peta Lily. Recent designs include *Angels in America* for Unity Theatre; *The Corrupted Angel* for Base Chorus; *Tmesis* and *Memento Mori* for Momentum Theatre Company; *Sacred Move* for Chaturangan South Asian Dance at Liverpool Anglican Cathedral and *Gallery*, a site-specific work with Chapter 4 Dance Company. Phil is currently Technical Manager at Unity Theatre, Liverpool.

Angela Simpson (Designer)

Angela joined The Chicken Shed Theatre Company as a teenager but learnt relatively quickly that she was happier backstage. She studied Fine Art at Middlesex University before completing the Motley Theatre Design Course. Angela's design work includes *The Baby and Fly Pie, Basil & Beattie* and *Habitat* (Royal Exchange Studio); *The Pocket Dream* and *The Derby McQueen Affair* (York Theatre Royal); *Under the Curse* and *Habitats* (The Gate);

Unsung/Consuming Songs (BAC); *The Danny Crowe Show* (Dundee Rep); *Komb* (National Theatre Studio); *L'Enfant et les Sortileges* and *L'Heure Espanol* (RSAMD), *Crime and Punishment in Dalston (*Arcola Theatre); *Bread and Butter* (Southwark Playhouse); *Change of Heart* (New End Theatre); *Comedy of Errors* (Oval House); *A Midsummer Night's Dream, Extension Treble Zero, Anansi* and *Boubile* (Chicken Shed Theatre Company); *Royalty* (So Loose Films). Angela is currently designing *Darwin's Dream,* a children's music show, which is touring before being performed at the Royal Albert Hall in 2006. Angela also curates Wallace Space Gallery in Covent Garden. A portfolio of her work can be seen at www.angelasimpson.com

Brian Docherty (Composer)

Brian wrote the music for Ronan O'Donnell's play *Brazil* in 2003 and most recently composed for Paines Plough's production of Douglas Maxwell's *If Destroyed True.* As the main protagonist behind Scientific Support Dept., Brian is currently working on a new project *Serf*, which will see the release of their debut album in 2006. Previous works with director Graeme Maley include *Macbeth* and *The Danny Crowe Show.*

Jennifer De Ornellas (Stage Manager)

Jennifer trained at Hope Street Ltd on their physical theatre programme. Since leaving Hope Street she has been involved in a wide variety of creative activities including setting up Capricho Puppet Company; Deputy Stage Manager on *Angels in America* directed by Lee Beagley; Stage Manager for Brouhaha's Merseyside International Street Festival; Stage Manager for Liverpool Culture Company's flagship project *It's Not OK;* Stage Manager for Hope Street's trading arm Culture Inc. which produced *Golden Slipper.* Jennifer is also part of Merseyside International Carnival Crew, working alongside the notorious designer Ray Allen Mahabir. She has also assisted the infamous Alan Richardson in the coordination of Hope Street's Theatre, Culture and Community Programme.

The Doll Tower by Ronan O'Donnell is a beautifully poetic play inviting history to discuss a contemporary problem. Thematically swallowing its iconic protagonist and spitting out theatricality as an end in itself, this play, like all great art, reflects back to us our complexities, our actions and their conclusion.

Graeme Maley, August 2005

 Liverpool's
New Writing
Theatre

Writer in Residence   Chris Fittock
General Manager   Nicki Green
Artistic Director   Graeme Maley
Literary Assistant   Sharon Sephton

www.lltnewwriting.com

For their help and support in the production of *The Doll Tower*, LLT would like to thank Arts Council England North West, Liverpool Culture Company, all the staff at Unity Theatre Liverpool, JMU Liverpool, Robert Longthorn, Andy Pettener from Flat 13 Design, Sharon Sephton, Brian Walton, Garfield Weston Foundation, The Peggy Ramsay Foundation, Seven Pillars of Wisdom Trust, Imperial War Museum London, Royal Liverpool Philharmonic and Nick Hern for choosing to publish *The Doll Tower*.

LLT would particularly like to thank David Llewellyn of JMU Liverpool for his support in the production of *The Doll Tower*.

EUROPEAN CAPITAL OF CULTURE

The work of LLT, Liverpool's New Writing Theatre, would not be possible without generous support from Arts Council England North West and Liverpool Culture Company.

THE DOLL TOWER

Ronan O'Donnell

Characters

LOWELL THOMAS, *an American journalist*

T.E. LAWRENCE/SHAW, *small thin man, elusive*

BRUCE, *eighteen-year-old Aberdonian*

UXBRIDGE, *petty criminal*

RUDE, *young and keen on being a soldier*

M.O., *the Medical Officer, veteran of the Great War*

CORPORAL INGLIS, *a Glaswegian, veteran of the Great War*

This text went to press before the end of rehearsals so may differ slightly from the play as performed.

ACT ONE

Scene One

The stage of the Royal Opera House, Covent Garden, 1920. A clutter of bogus oriental sets. There is a chair and stand with a glass and jug of lemonade. LOWELL THOMAS *in a dinner suit. He is preparing for the performance he will give later on that evening.*

THOMAS. My lords, ladies and gentlemen. Good evening and welcome to one of the most extraordinary tales of heroism the modern world has ever witnessed. Tonight, through the power of motion film, I will take you on the most extraordinary journey. Walk with me . . . em . . . walk with me . . . damn it. Walk with me. Where's the . . . ? Harry, run the film, will ya? Run the film. Walk with me as we recreate . . . as we conjure here on the stage of Covent Garden the waterless deserts of Arabia and the red sandstone bastions of the Wadi Rum, sun-scorched and silent as the moon. Silent, that is, until the engine of war began to whine its horrible mechanical song. Only in this theatre of conflict the droning fighter plane is accompanied by the drum beat of camel-mounted regiments of wild Bedouin. For far from the Western front and its stagnant trench-warfare, another more fluid battle was being waged in the Holy Land of three world religions. The Allied war against the Turks was led by two men of outstanding character. It is their story I am here to tell. They are the cut of men that only great empires sire. In what has been called the Last Crusade . . .

LAWRENCE (*clapping* THOMAS). The Last Crusade? How droll.

THOMAS. Well, well. Look who it is.

LAWRENCE. Turn it off. I think I've seen and heard enough.

THOMAS. Harry, cut the film. You of all people. How come I ain't surprised?

LAWRENCE. I was wondering, the other day . . .

THOMAS. The mysterious Colonel Lawrence.

LAWRENCE. . . . about how quickly the war has been turned into a peep-show entertainment.

THOMAS. People ain't ready for normalcy. The war is too fresh . . . too raw in here.

LAWRENCE. The set. It's *Moonlight on the Nile*?

THOMAS. Yeah, they were throwing it out. Run ended. I bought it off them for a song.

LAWRENCE. It all sounds very Valentino – *The Son of the Sheik*.

THOMAS. You're embarrassed?

LAWRENCE. It's all so very picturesque.

THOMAS. That's what Lloyd George said. 'The most picturesque man of our era.' That's a direct quote. The man is in awe of you.

LAWRENCE. It's full of inaccuracies.

THOMAS. I guess so. It's a personal take . . . Back home the whole of New York was agog. Hey, the show's a sell-out. They want to extend the run.

LAWRENCE. Rather unfortunate phrase: 'sell out'.

THOMAS. You did your best, T.E.. Feisal has no better friend.

LAWRENCE. That is not how they see me.

THOMAS. I know you're sensitive.

LAWRENCE. Am I?

THOMAS. But people are fascinated. You can't stop that. The whole of London wants to meet you. You're hot property.

LAWRENCE. That is why I've come to see you.

THOMAS. Where are you hiding? I tried to find you. Soon as I got off the boat I was working the lines.

LAWRENCE. You, my dear Lowell, are making my life a misery.

THOMAS. You're not sleeping rough, are you? You look a bit worn round the edges.

LAWRENCE. As a result of your . . . what's it called?

THOMAS. It's called an illustrated cinematic lecture, old boy.

LAWRENCE. As a result of your entertainment, I'm being hounded night and day.

THOMAS. I'll get you a ticket.

LAWRENCE. If it's not autograph-fiends . . .

THOMAS. . . . put you on the guest list.

LAWRENCE. . . . then it's reporters, magazine editors and, dare I say, representatives of the gentler sex.

THOMAS. Dames? You mean women.

LAWRENCE. Yes – those.

THOMAS. Oh, T.E., I bet you'd rather mix it with a whole Turk army corps.

LAWRENCE. Give me the desert any day.

THOMAS. Play cricket with your tulip bombs.

LAWRENCE. To lie 'under the canopy of stars with thy brothers of the black tents.' Do you know, I've received twenty-eight proposals of marriage?

THOMAS. How the hell do they find you? No one else can. And that's the best news-hounds in England. I know.

LAWRENCE. They arrive . . . via Oxford. By mail. Mostly.

THOMAS. Twenty-eight proposals. See the influence of this cinema gizmo? I'm telling you, this is big.

LAWRENCE. I'm being followed.

THOMAS. You're being what?

LAWRENCE. Tailed – isn't that what you Americans call it?

THOMAS. Tailed. Shadowed. Do you know who by?

LAWRENCE. I've moved time and again but my shadow always finds me.

THOMAS. Are you positive?

LAWRENCE. I'm not a complete paranoid invert.

THOMAS. You need to get a good look at the guy. My advice. Let the guy know you've marked him.

LAWRENCE. We have indeed met face to face. And it's not a man, Lowell, it's a woman.

THOMAS. What?

LAWRENCE. A lady. An Italian lady.

THOMAS. Don't say?

LAWRENCE. An Italian countess, to be precise.

THOMAS. Let me get this right. You're being tailed by an Italian aristocrat? Wow, you got style.

LAWRENCE. She happens to be a countess. She wears a wristwatch on her ankle.

THOMAS. You're kidding me.

LAWRENCE. I must be out of London. Everywhere is closing in on me.

THOMAS. Here. Have a lemonade.

LAWRENCE. I want a halt called to this charade. Lowell, I order you to close down this production.

THOMAS. Now hold on.

LAWRENCE. I want it closed down immediately.

THOMAS. Lawrence, there's no prospect of me sailing for America tomorrow or next month. I've signed a contract. You understand? I put it together solely for an American audience . . .

LAWRENCE. Well, it's over here now – damned it. It's full of lies.

THOMAS. That's not so.

LAWRENCE. I will not be imprisoned in a lie.

THOMAS. If anything's way-out, I'll gladly amend it. Come on. Don't you want to see Abu Tayi and all the rest of the Arabian knights on the big screen? Those Arabs were our allies. Allenby's right flank. The side-show of a side-show that's packing them in. Full houses, every night.

LAWRENCE. No doubt it's a great hoot.

THOMAS. They look splendid. Sit down. Let's watch the rest of it. Harry!

LAWRENCE. You Americans know nothing of the Arabs.

THOMAS. Yeah? I'll tell you what I do know. I read the papers and last month you British happened to use the RAF on that Cairo demonstration. And how many a month are being killed in Mesopotamia? Forty million pounds it's cost so far. Three times more gold than your Arab Revolt. The whole region's a mess.

LAWRENCE (*mimicking Churchill*). Yes, a melancholy and alarming picture.

THOMAS. You guys made promises.

LAWRENCE. Better to break our word than to lose.

THOMAS. I saw your letter in *The Times*. Hot stuff.

LAWRENCE. I intend to make England ashamed of itself, if I can.

THOMAS. Did the Paris Conference resolve anything at all? What's your opinion? (*Going for his press notebook.*)

LAWRENCE. The Arabs will not thank us. France's mendacious mandatory in Syria will not last. Mecca and Medina will be absorbed in a few years by an Arab state with Damascus as its capital. As cheap fuel in Mesopotamia begins to flow, the Arab centre will inevitably be transferred eastward to Mosul, Baghdad, or some new capital . . .

THOMAS. Listen. Hey, have a glass of lemonade. Are you all right? Why don't we watch some more?

LAWRENCE. Perhaps I should. Cinema is so vulgar. It will never catch on.

THOMAS. They said that about the electric light bulb. You should see Coney Island. Come on, sit down. You can dictate to me your comments.

LAWRENCE. Shall I?

THOMAS. I'll take notes. I want to get things right.

LAWRENCE. It's full of inventions.

THOMAS. The Big Picture can be a bit flat sometimes. It needs a bit of colour to hurry it along. You know what I mean? What was it Foch said, Marshal Foch, about how he won the war?

LAWRENCE. 'By smoking my pipe.' That's what he said.

THOMAS. There. You see. You can't show two hours of an old man puffing a pipe. Likewise the Western Front's a bit too – how shall we say? – mud-coloured.

LAWRENCE. The necessary supply of heroes must be maintained at all cost.

THOMAS. The war didn't end on the eleventh hour of the eleventh day of the eleventh month, Lawrence. The war goes on, in here.

LAWRENCE. I want you to print in the programme an acknowledgement that Colonel Lawrence is not, repeat *not* the source . . .

THOMAS. Why?

LAWRENCE. . . . from which the facts of this cinematic production were obtained nor, *nor* is he in any way responsible for its contents.

THOMAS. You think this a post-war morale booster? Maybe it is. Maybe . . . it goes deeper than that. Folks looking for an answer. Millions dead, Lawrence. Young men drowning in mud holes without firing one lousy shot in anger. You're an emotional pill makes the old man feel proud. You're the kind of guy an empire needs. I hear them weeping out there. And yeah, it shakes me up. As far as they're concerned, you're a hero. A real Arabian Knight.

LAWRENCE. It was all an act.

THOMAS. All I know is it works.

LAWRENCE. You see, I know how false the praise is . . .

THOMAS. I don't how it works but it sure does.

LAWRENCE. . . . how little reality compared with the legend; how much luck, how little merit.

THOMAS. You're a hero, T.E. Who fought the war? The masses did and now they need a hero. But they can't imagine one for themselves.

LAWRENCE. That's your vocation, is it?

THOMAS. The little guy wants to be part of a story. We give him a story, make him part of the big picture. Don't you think we have a duty to make sure the world goes in the right direction? I mean, that's what you tried . . . wasn't it?

LAWRENCE. So Colonel Lawrence marches on, only I have stepped out of the way.

THOMAS. I can't get over you guys. You Europeans.

LAWRENCE. But it's all lies.

THOMAS. Come on, Lawrence, you told me yourself . . . in Cairo. In the bar of the Continental: 'History is not made up of the truth, so why worry?' Why worry? (*They both laugh.*) You taught me that.

LAWRENCE. Did I?

THOMAS. Come on. Sit down.

LAWRENCE. You will publish that retraction?

THOMAS. Of course . . . Hey, it's great to see you. Where you staying?

LAWRENCE. In rooms.

THOMAS. In rooms? Where?

LAWRENCE. Above the Dover Street underground. (*Giggles.*) My landlady thinks I work as a shoe salesman. Frightful place, but cheap.

THOMAS. I won't tell anyone.

LAWRENCE. I beg you not to.

THOMAS. You up to something?

LAWRENCE. What do you mean?

THOMAS. Stuff I heard. Never mind. Come round tomorrow. For dinner. The Ritz. Meet Lucy.

LAWRENCE. Lucy?

THOMAS. My wife.

LAWRENCE. You're married?

THOMAS. Sure am. She's some kid. She opens the show. We do the Dance of the Seven Veils then she does a number. She sings that call to prayer . . . The muezzin's call to prayer. Her own composition. She's very artistic. Wait till you meet her. Made an honest man of me. (LAWRENCE *picks up his books and makes to exit.*) Take it easy, T.E. She's not about to enter stage left. She's out and about. The Tower of London and all sights in-between. Another lemonade? I'll run some more film. Sit down. Please.

LAWRENCE. Do I want to?

THOMAS. You got an appointment elsewhere? Maybe your tailor. Get him run up some fancy robes.

LAWRENCE. Yes, a sherif of Mecca.

THOMAS. An Arabian Knight. Run the film, will ya? Harry.

We see more film. LAWRENCE *gets up, knocking his chair over and hurriedly exits.*

Lawrence! I don't get that guy. Comes begging me for his privacy, hates being in the limelight. Yeah, like a guy who walks backwards into the spotlight. Maybe I should re-jig my opening lines. (*Gets dramatic.*) At this moment, somewhere in London, hiding from a host of feminine admirers, book publishers, autograph hunters and every species of hero-worshipper, is a young man whose name will go down in history alongside those of Drake and Raleigh. Yeah. (*Picks up T.E.'s books.*) Persian poetry. *The Diary of a Disappointed Man.* Such preposterous creatures these Arabian Knights, huh? Nomads. Not fitted for ordinary society. *The Diary of a Disappointed Man.* Don't make me laugh. Don't make me laugh, T.E.

Scene Two

We see the year: 1923.

Bovington Training Camp of the Royal Tank Regiment. Interior of a barracks. A row of beds, lockers. A stove at one end. The CORPORAL *has his own office-cum-sleeping quarters leading into this space.* UXBRIDGE *is sitting on his bed playing a mouth organ.* RUDE *is showing* BRUCE *how to make a bed-block.* LAWRENCE, *now* T.E. SHAW, *is reading a book.* SHAW's *bed-block and kit lay-out is perfect.* CORPORAL INGLIS *is readying himself in his own space. There's a bicycle in his space. He looks at his fob watch, then surreptitiously pours himself a nip of whisky from a half-bottle taken from the drawer in his desk.*

RUDE (*folding an army blanket with* BRUCE). You grab that end.

BRUCE. I'm never gonny get this . . .

RUDE. Now turn it. Turn it then.

BRUCE. Which way?

RUDE. Wait a minute, prick. It's buff side up.

BRUCE. Who you calling a prick?

RUDE. I'm trying to help. Nap has to be right way round. Sheets to go in the middle bit. Fuckin rats' arses.

BRUCE. Bed-block's no something we do at home, mate. My maw's no big on them.

UXBRIDGE. You show him how it's done. Just you show him. (*To* SHAW.) Look at the state of that. He's wonderful dexterous, the boy. It ain't a turban. Might as well be. It's a blanket, not a whatsit. What's he doing with it? Look at him. (*Laughs.*)

BRUCE. Dinny heed him.

RUDE. That's Uxbridge. Gripes noon and night. Big gob-bucket. He doesn't want to be a soldier.

UXBRIDGE. Rookie's waltz. Sar' Major's goat's pissed on parade.

RUDE. Is this the right way round? Let me think.

BRUCE. How the fuck you do your own?

UXBRIDGE. He popped it out – like a great big woolly egg.

RUDE. I fuckin know how to do mine, mate.

UXBRIDGE. Don't worry, Jock – time your basic's finished you'll whop it together between a shave an a shit.

BRUCE. Is it no the same?

RUDE. Naw. Ma bed's over there an I'm facing the other way round. Look.

BRUCE. Right.

RUDE. See what I mean?

BRUCE. Naw.

UXBRIDGE. God help the Empire. He's not very spatially aware is Rude. They won't let him near the range. The instructors are terrified of him. He's trashed a three tonner already. Scolded a Paddy the other day, in the canteen. Came charging through the door. Paddy's got a bun in his mouth and a mug of tea in each hand. He's up the sick bay – more bandages than fucking Tutankhamen . . .

RUDE. Nothing up with my fucking motoring.

UXBRIDGE. We're no talking of your motoring, dipstick. It's your braking technique that's under the microscope. He asked the wrong man. Should have asked your mate.

BRUCE. He's no my mate.

UXBRIDGE. In't he? Yous were awfully pally last night when yous got in.

BRUCE. You the hut stickybeak?

UXBRIDGE. Sitting there whispering away in the dark . . . Stickybeak? Got to keep your eyes peeled round here, mate. What's your name, Jock? All sorts of rotten ones round here. Army's the home of scum. Mollys. Mollys you can't tell is Mollys. Built like brick out-houses. They say that boxing instructor – him Rude – he's a Molly. You ain't a Molly, is ya?

BRUCE. What you on about – what's a Molly?

UXBRIDGE. Just don't bend over in the showers, Jock. That's all I'm saying. Soap slops out your hand, don't go fucking looking for it. Or it won't be length of rhubarb growing out the cheeks of your arse.

RUDE. Take a bite out my bum and call me a fucking apple.

UXBRIDGE (*standing in awe of* SHAW*'s bed-block and kit*). For a first try this is fuckin tip-top. How'd you do that? A'm sayin how'd you do that? I've been here near a month and there's not a bloke in this pig's billet can manage that. Done like a right old stager. Who showed you that, then?

SHAW. Sorry. You said something? I was somewhere else.

UXBRIDGE. Oh yeah. Where was you, then?

SHAW. A rather long way away.

UXBRIDGE (*takes the book*). Meso . . . Meso-po-fucking-tania?

RUDE. Here, is that your bike out there?

UXBRIDGE. Got flappers in it?

RUDE. Come look at this chap's 'bus'.

UXBRIDGE. Molly's more like.

BRUCE. Will you lay off?

UXBRIDGE. I'm impressed wi the kit lay-out. That's all. How you do it?

SHAW. The house organ, old boy.

UXBRIDGE. The house organ? Is that not that big piano up the picture house? Rises up out the orchestra pit?

SHAW. King's regulations. In the house organ.

UXBRIDGE. We ain't crap-hats . . . this is the Tanks.

SHAW. There's a diagram. Very salutary. House organ's a must for the new recruit.

UXBRIDGE. He keeps sayin organ – I'm puttin in for a hut transfer.

BRUCE. It's a gazette . . . *The Army Quarterly*. A read it on the train, on the way doon. A seen it maself. Didn't I, mister?

UXBRIDGE. Slow down, Jock – you two join up together?

BRUCE. You can pick up a copy in the library o the Union Jack club.

UXBRIDGE. Union Jack got a library?

SHAW. A very good one.

UXBRIDGE. It's got a smashing bar. Never heard tell of an actual library. The only books in that place is a few sailors wi filth make yer eyes water. Oriental stuff, i'n it?

RUDE. They say French is choice filth.

UXBRIDGE. Never heard of a library in the Union Jack.

BRUCE. It's got a library a'right.

RUDE. There, it's fuckin done. (*Admiring the bed-block.*) Work of a fuckin skilled tradesman.

BRUCE. Ta much. I'm no cut out for this mince.

UXBRIDGE. Can't make you out, Jock. Strange guttural accent you've got. Never mind – you'll do well in the Punjab.

SHAW. Shouldn't think we'll be posted anywhere near the frontier when we finish basic training.

UXBRIDGE. Don't say?

SHAW. Tanks aren't suited to mountainous terrain. Light mountain guns. Mule-mounted infantry and transports. That's the kit you'd need. Tanks would be useless there.

RUDE. There. (*Referring to the bed-block.*) What you think?

BRUCE. It's a bit lop-sided.

SHAW. Of course, a soldier has to go where he's sent.

UXBRIDGE. Yeah, at the double.

SHAW. Regardless.

UXBRIDGE. Sleep 1, 2, 3. Shave 1, 2, 3. Crap 1, 2 . . .

SHAW. He is owned by the state. A servile condition made no less so by being voluntary.

UXBRIDGE. No one owns me. No even that pig of a corporal.

SHAW. Oh come, sir . . .

UXBRIDGE. Sir?

SHAW. Slaves would be free, if they could be. They would escape at the first opportunity. But the soldier assigns to his owner the twenty-four-hour use of his body. The mentality of ordinary human slaves must be terrible, but a soldier by his own act is drained of volition, like dead leaves in the wind.

UXBRIDGE. Slaves don't get pay. They don't go down the pub. Don't go out on the randan.

RUDE. The scrumpy's foxy round here. The blackouts are terrific.

SHAW. It's hardly pay . . . more like pocket money. Worth and labour are waived, surely, in the soldier's contract.

UXBRIDGE. You've lost me, mate.

RUDE. My daydream was to be a soldier. Women always pick soldier boys. These is the best togs I've ever worn. Flaunt it, I say.

SHAW. Only women with a pimp are interested in this uniform.

UXBRIDGE. Where'd you pick him up, Jock? He starts reciting fancy verses, if he doesn't talk proper – I'll go to the glass house for him.

SHAW. I'm sorry if my speech offends you.

UXBRIDGE. He's taking the micky. Hey, Rude, we got a professor in the hut. Swallowed a bleedin dictionary. This hut's rep is mud.

BRUCE (*taking* SHAW *aside*). Best to not talk too much. Low profile.

SHAW. Have I made another enemy? He seems a likable sort.

BRUCE. No need to play games.

SHAW. It is a mean game that's played with me. You have your instructions.

BRUCE. I've to watch you don't come to any harm, sir.

14

SHAW. He has spies everywhere.

BRUCE. Not fuckin here?

SHAW. Yes. Here. Have I not shown you the extent of his reach? The Old Man gave away my hiding place before. Fame has placed a price on my head, a rope around my neck, this he knows. He would follow me to the hermit caves of Syria such is his . . . He is implacable.

BRUCE. Is there no other way you can pay him back, sir?

SHAW. No. This barrack is to be my life. A common soldier manacled in this chain gang.

BRUCE. How long have you to stay?

SHAW. The Old Man decides. Until we know more fully his plans, we both must be careful and discreet. He has buried me in the shallow grave of duty. I have no choice if my name is not to be dragged through the mire.

BRUCE. I can be discreet, sir, but can you? You stick out like a sore thumb. Yer patter marks you.

SHAW. You were warned the task would not be easy. That you would be tested.

BRUCE. I gave my word of honour.

SHAW. I have a new name now. Only you know the secret which makes my life joyless. Do not try to help me too much. We will put a distance between us. So as not to attract attention.

BRUCE. They're already talking about us.

RUDE *and* UXBRIDGE *are talking in low tones.*

SHAW. Knuckle down to being ordinary, that was his last order.

UXBRIDGE (*walks over to* SHAW *and blows smoke right in his face*). Got any fags on you, Professor?

SHAW *produces them.* UXBRIDGE *takes them.*

CORPORAL INGLIS *enters briskly, fob watch in hand.* RUDE *and* UXBRIDGE *dash for their beds.*

INGLIS. Stand by your beds. M.O.'s inspection in five minutes. Uxbridge, put out that fuckin fag. Any of you laddies let me down wi yer oxter and foot hygiene, I'll be sticking you on the fucking crap patrol wi a toothbrush and a bar o carbolic. You, Rude, how's your oxter and foot hygiene?

RUDE. Fine, Corporal.

INGLIS. Sunny is the word, Rude. Not 'fine'. This hut, my hut will go down in the ruddy annals. Mentioned at His Majesty's high table as they pass the cigars round. The King will turn to the French ambassador and in a quiet laconic manner boast o the foot and oxter hygiene in Corporal Inglis's hut. Your anus will sparkle like a brass Buddha. That is an order. Cleanliness is next to godliness. Any socialist slum-dweller . . .

SHAW. Socialist? What's wrong with socialists?

RUDE. My anus, Corp?

INGLIS. My anus, your anus, every fuckin would-be trooper in this hut's anus – sparkly like a brass Buddha. Ever been in Malaysia, son? Loads of Buddhas. Polished brass – magnificent sight. That's the benchmark.

SHAW. Corporal.

INGLIS. Yes . . . Shaw.

SHAW. My uniform's a bit on the large side . . . do you think I can have a change?

INGLIS. Quartermaster has only two sizes, laddie, too large and too small. And anyway, army with the smartest uniform always loses. You'll do.

M.O. *enters, wearing his white coat over his officer's uniform and carrying a clipboard with notes attached.*

Attention! Name and number to the officer. Sir.

M.O. Thank you, Corporal. (*Goes to* UXBRIDGE.)

UXBRIDGE. Uxbridge. Zero-3989, sir.

M.O. How's the teeth, Uxbridge?

UXBRIDGE. Very well, sir. Gums have left off being sore, sir.

M.O. Wide open, wide open. (*Looks in his mouth.*) And the feet?

UXBRIDGE. Top nick, sir.

INGLIS. Drop yer breeks.

UXBRIDGE *drops his trousers.*

M.O. Free from infection, Corporal.

INGLIS (*writes on his clipboard*). F.F.I. He's finished 'is T.C.P. course an all, sir. Lice-free.

M.O. Good. Excellent news. (*Moves on to* RUDE.)

INGLIS. Pull them back up, then.

RUDE. Rude. 5498-zero, sir.

M.O. Corporal. Isn't this the chap – slightly malnourished?

INGLIS. That's the boy, sir. Drop yer breeks. Looking a lot better, isn't he, sir?

M.O. Yes, much better. How are you coping with basic training? Not too taxing?

RUDE. It's smoother than ploughing clay morning till night, sir.

INGLIS. 'Mazing what a purpose in life and three meals a day does, sir.

M.O. Free from infection. Feet?

RUDE. Feet's grand, sir. (M.O. *moves on to* BRUCE.)

INGLIS. This the new intake, sir. Him and him, sir.

M.O. New intake? I thought this course had already started?

INGLIS. Search me, sir. His notes are there, sir. Name and number to the officer. And say 'sir' when replying.

BRUCE. 78757. John. Bruce, sir.

M.O. Any health problems, Bruce? Teeth, feet, (*Coughs.*) hygiene?

INGLIS. Drop yer breeks, laddie. Stand up straight.

BRUCE. None that I ken . . . sir.

M.O. How were you employed before you joined up?

BRUCE. Nightclub doorman, sir. In London. Before that I had a spell on trawlers, sir. Aberdeen, sir.

INGLIS. Your kit's a disgrace.

BRUCE. I'm just through the door.

INGLIS. Don't answer back. Sorry, sir.

M.O. Quite alright, Corporal. Free from infection.

INGLIS. Who told yi tae pull yer trousers back up, Bruce?

BRUCE. I didn't know . . .

INGLIS. You can pull them up noo.

M.O. *moves on to* SHAW.

SHAW. T.E. Shaw. 78756, sir. (*Drops his trousers.*)

M.O. Any problems? Teeth, feet, (*Coughs.*) hygiene?

SHAW. None, sir. I have as much quinine as I need.

M.O. Quinine? You've had malaria? Where did you . . . ?

SHAW. Out east, sir. Palestine.

M.O. You were in the Great War?

SHAW. No, sir. Civilian Detainee. Ottomans interned me at
    Constantinople. Fine chaps, sir. No maltreatment. Really quite
    an easy war, sir.

INGLIS. We dinny all have easy wars, did we, sir?

M.O. No, we didn't. Must say, being interned in Constantinople
    sounds just the ticket. Free from infection. (*The* M.O. *spots
    some books in* SHAW*'s locker.*) You read this sort of stuff,
    Shaw?

SHAW. Yes, sir.

INGLIS. Pull yer breeks up, laddie, when the officer's talking tae yi.

M.O. *The Principles of War* by Marshal Foch. It's in French.

SHAW. Strategy interests me, sir. Foch in particular. The French
    cult of the offensive. Plan 17 was, as you know, a total disaster.

M.O. Quite.

SHAW. Strategy 'war on a map' is quite different from the
    improvisations of irregular troops. The experts are always
    preparing for the last war. Foch forgets Nelson's maxim that
    'An officer must have political courage.'

INGLIS. There's nae politics in the Tanks, sir. Politics is socialism,
    sir.

M.O. What were you at before you joined up?

SHAW. An architect's office, sir.

M.O. An architect's office? You've signed up for seven years. What
    possessed you to join up?

SHAW. I don't quite know, sir. I think chiefly for some mental rest.

M.O. What?

SHAW. Mental rest, sir.

M.O. Pardon? What do you mean, mental rest?

SHAW. Or, or perhaps I'm simply having a nervous breakdown, sir.

M.O. What? Corporal, take this man's name. Gross impertinence! (M.O. *exits.*)

INGLIS. Yes, sir. You lot remain at attention.

He follows the M.O. *The men remain at attention.*

RUDE. Fuck sake.

UXBRIDGE. Lads. The professor has dumped us right in it.

RUDE. Inglis will bandy our ballocks in barbed wire.

UXBRIDGE. Confined to barracks.

RUDE. White Horse is out of bounds.

UXBRIDGE. The crap patrol.

BRUCE. Did you have to?

UXBRIDGE. Thank you very much, Shaw.

BRUCE. Isny a lark this.

UXBRIDGE. You little fucking creep.

RUDE. He's queer alright.

UXBRIDGE. Stuffed if I'm eating sawdust for that shit. Foch an 'is strategy. Plan 17. What's he . . . ?

RUDE. White Horse out of bounds.

UXBRIDGE. Fuckin outrageous.

INGLIS (*enters. Goes straight to* SHAW). Ever had your nose at the bottom o a fire bucket? There is 822 fire buckets in this fuckin camp. You will clean and dub each one. Rude.

RUDE. Yes, Corp.

INGLIS. You will be this comedian's fuckin assistant.

RUDE. Why me, Corp?

INGLIS (*to* RUDE). Get into your scruffs. Shaw, I know your type. I can smell socialist. Not slum-dweller socialist but high-class fanny socialist. Socialist what's got a bleeding heart. Socialist what goes to the opera and ne'er thinks twice about the coachman left sitting outside in the freezing snaw. Socialism that drinks wine – a single bottle costs a year's pay to a fuckin scrunt like Uxbridge. Well, you are in the Tanks, sonny. Welcome to the brotherhood whose common fare is puke and sweat and graft. It's the monkey wrench no the fucking hotel lounge newspapers. You'll no be wearing your smoking jacket in this billet. Uxbridge and you, Bruce. Thirty press-ups on the double.

INGLIS *slowly walks round the ramrod straight towards* SHAW.

Scene Three

The barracks. UXBRIDGE *and* RUDE *are beating up* SHAW *in his bed.* BRUCE *is asleep.* INGLIS *is in his room with a mug of whisky in his hand.*

UXBRIDGE. Hey Professor, psst, Professor. Here's a book for you. A nudey book.

RUDE. Big titties an that.

UXBRIDGE. Fucking nuns, torn bloomers, the lot.

INGLIS. Silence in the barracks!

UXBRIDGE *and* RUDE *return to their beds.* BRUCE *gets out of bed and sits closer to* SHAW.

SHAW. Don't touch me . . . (*Reading as he writes.*) Dear Robert, you say I do not enjoy a good conscience. It's true. Perhaps there is not enough art in my own self-deceptions. Everyone else has forged for themselves a little peace. Not I. I am mendacious, artificial and untransparent. I hide. It seems not to arouse too much suspicion. No one has rumbled my disguise. So I have stopped digging. I have put aside my spade. I don't know why here in particular in this hard army life. In this doss-house I've struck bedrock among the lumpen proletariat. But something of here has an echo of the desert about it. I can smell the mustiness of the cave-dweller about me. The hermit smell. The unclean hermit smell of an emaciated man whose very body, what's left of it, is an act of concealment. Whose face and wisdom is a hiding-place and a mask. (*Stops writing.*) Do not look into the hermit's shining eyes, Corporal. They will not be laughing at you. But at the terrible things licensed by sadistic routine. How will I serve my new comrades? These men that seem to come

from another race. How will I do my pretend stuff? My filthy
trickster routines? Hoots. (*He giggles.*) My new name is T.E.
Shaw. Do write back and don't be alarmed. Love to all.

He blows the candle out.

Scene Four

SHAW *is scrubbing the barrack floor.* CORPORAL INGLIS *is
standing over him with a pick-shaft handle. The other men are also
scrubbing.*

INGLIS. Number one: leaving overalls on your bed is contrary to
King's Regulations. You've been here three weeks and still you
can't get it fuckin right, laddie. Number two: do not ever let me
catch you removing insignia from your uniform again. How's
Tanks meant to know you're a wee insignificant shite? What
kind of regiment you think this is? Rank is everything. This is
no jolly rest cure. That bike you run around in. I don't like Flash
Harrys. Flash Harrys might impress the rest o the local
population but they do not impress me. Keep scrubbing! What's
this, refusing to salute an officer?

SHAW. I did not refuse to salute an officer.

INGLIS. You did so.

SHAW. It was he who refused to return my salute.

INGLIS. He's a 'effin Major. Major can pee in your pocket if he's
so inclined. Major's ruddy livid, you digging him up. He's livid,
laddie.

SHAW. The salute is paid not to the man but to the rank.

INGLIS. Speechless, he is. Speechless.

SHAW. And the officer saluted is ordered by the King, whom he
represents, to return the salute.

INGLIS. Going through the camp like a dose of ruddy salts.

SHAW. I'm sure you know the relevant King's Regulations,
Corporal.

INGLIS. Tell me something, Shaw. You got some suicide wish?
The other huts won't let you forget this. You got tongues
wagging. Who's the runt in hut F12, N.C.Os are asking? Forgets

to wear insignia. Turns right instead of left on parade. Mucking up our lovely drill. Men laughing. Laughing in the ranks. It's fuckin unheard of. Your life will be misery.

SHAW. I do not grumble at my fate, Corporal.

INGLIS (*showing scissors*). You know what these are?

SHAW. They appear to be scissors, Corporal.

INGLIS. They appear to be . . . They're special scissors. Not ordinary. Special regimental scissors for cutting the heads off dandelions. That's right. The lawn outside the officers' mess is ablaze with them. A most unmilitary sight. Nature dumping her bounty willy-nilly. I won't have it, Shaw. I simply . . . Each and every dandelion head chopped off at regulation height. Got it, laddie?

SHAW. Yes, Corporal.

INGLIS. This is no picnic. Over there, get cutting.

SHAW. What about the Celandine?

INGLIS. What?

SHAW. Lesser Celandine to be precise. *Ranunculus ficaria*. It flowers soon. I see a smattering of them on the lawn. Round the hedges. Do you want me to snip those too? Regulation height.

INGLIS. You think you know everything. A real mine of antique information. Get cutting. Get cutting!

RUDE. It's freezing, Corp.

INGLIS (*to* SHAW). Smarmy bastard.

UXBRIDGE. It's fuckin Baltic, Corp.

INGLIS *stands on his fingers.*

INGLIS. Get on with it. Mind the . . . what's it called? What's it called, Shaw?

SHAW. *Ranunculus ficaria.*

INGLIS. Mind the Runty-cunty-fellatio, to give it its full Latin fuckin name. It's a delicate spring flower. Like you, shower.

M.O. *enters.*

M.O. Corporal.

INGLIS. Sa!

M.O. A word, please. (*To* INGLIS.) That man, Shaw. I want you to keep an especial eye on him.

INGLIS. I've got my eye on him, sir. You can be sure of that.

M.O. You will be discreet.

INGLIS. Discreet, sir? I'm not sure I know what you mean, sir.

M.O. The C.O. wishes a report.

INGLIS. Sir.

M.O. Regular notices. You will report to me. Note his moods. And if he's writing anything. His nerves are not to be taxed too far.

INGLIS. It's my nerves, sir, he's taxed. He's very waspish, sir. Facetious. He's not fitted for the Tanks.

M.O. That may be so.

INGLIS. Nor I suspect for any society, sir. Unamendable will he has, sir. Loopy.

M.O. Loopy is not in my medical dictionary, Corporal.

INGLIS. Not that he's a lounger like Uxbridge. Give him a task and belts right into it, sir. Meticulous done, sir. Facetiously so.

M.O. Are you saying if he performs a job flawlessly it's a form of insubordination?

INGLIS. Absolutely so, sir.

M.O. I take it his attitude to his superiors lacks somewhat?

INGLIS. Ill done, sir. Ill done. He spits on it, sir. On the crown, sir. It's more than flesh and blood can stand, sir.

M.O. Do not strike him, Corporal – ever. Do you understand?

INGLIS. I've felt like it, sir.

M.O. Not a finger on him.

INGLIS. I've drew back my fist a couple of times.

M.O. Well, you will refrain – the C.O. is taking a personal interest in Shaw.

INGLIS. It's his eyes, sir.

M.O. His eyes? I'm not sure I'm with you, Inglis.

INGLIS. A right far-keeker, sir.

M.O. Speak English, Inglis.

INGLIS. Horrible blue eyes . . . like bits of sky through the eye-holes of a skull. Sir.

M.O. Don't be so disconcerting, Inglis. Carry on.

INGLIS. Sir.

M.O. *exits.*

Horrible blue eyes. Always watchin. Always following. Horrible.

Scene Five

Evening. UXBRIDGE *and* SHAW *are the only two left in the hut.* UXBRIDGE *has removed his tunic . . . puts a lump of coal in the stove.* SHAW *is reading and taking notes.*

UXBRIDGE. You satisfied now? Well made up, eh?

SHAW. To what are you referring?

UXBRIDGE. I don't know what you're trying to prove, Professor.

SHAW. I'm not trying to prove anything.

UXBRIDGE. You're doing everything wrong . . .

SHAW. It would be interesting . . .

UXBRIDGE. . . . deliberate.

SHAW. . . . if my actions justified something.

UXBRIDGE. There you go again.

SHAW. I'm afraid all they do is vouch for my peculiarity.

UXBRIDGE. Spouting off that well-read piss.

SHAW. I am determined to be myself . . . which is what? Nothing marks me as special. I don't have mystical eyeballs or great physical strength.

UXBRIDGE. Like you swallowed a fuckin vat full of Greek words. Why can't you slag NORMAL?

SHAW. What justifies you, Uxbridge? Why is one so disdainful of authority wearing that uniform? You intrigue me. Are you here to hide, or perhaps to drown something? Drown remorse?

UXBRIDGE. I ain't hiding. I've got nothing to fucking hide.

SHAW. The only consolation in this world is that there are some who love the damned.

UXBRIDGE. You sound like some French fuckin tart.

SHAW. All I say is never be too long alone with yourself.

UXBRIDGE. You're trying to say I'm a Molly. That's it. You are. You're trying to say . . .

SHAW *laughs*.

SHAW (*mocking*). Oh, you guessed my secret. Yes, I worship you, Uxbridge. Can't you tell? I worship the way you snore your fat head off.

UXBRIDGE. You keep your fuckin distance.

SHAW. I love your socks. I worship you the more you flee from me.

UXBRIDGE. You taking the cunt?

SHAW. Oh Uxbridge . . . be cold . . . be cruel . . . be criminal.

UXBRIDGE. You fuckin Nancy. You fucking Nancy!

CORPORAL INGLIS *enters*.

INGLIS. Do I hear voices raised in altercation? Huh? Did I hear the 'Nancy' word bandied? Cook not putting enough saltpetre in the tea? I'll have to have a word wi him. There'll be no shenanigans in my hut.

UXBRIDGE. Shenanigans. What shenanigans?

INGLIS. You not cleaning your kit? That's the only hobby a soldier needs. Believe me. You feel the urge, Uxbridge, down below . . . bull your boots. Look after your putees and base thoughts will keep clear. (*He pulls his cigs out.*) Uxbridge, you out of Woodbines?

UXBRIDGE. Actually . . . I am.

INGLIS. Tough. You want tae do what we did in the trenches.

UXBRIDGE. And what's that, Corp?

INGLIS. Get some horse-hair from your mattress – roll it in a bit of newspaper. It's a braw smoke. (*Walks past them towards his own room, smoking.*)

SHAW. Corporal?

INGLIS. What is it?

SHAW. May I have a word? I've been meaning to ask you. I'm writing . . .

INGLIS. I see that.

SHAW. I'm doing quite a bit, observations, etc., but the noise in here does knock my concentration. Especially late on.

INGLIS. Does it, laddie?

UXBRIDGE. Says I snore . . .

INGLIS. Shut up.

SHAW. I was wondering if I can apply for a single room?

UXBRIDGE. A single fuckin room.

INGLIS. A single room, yi say?

SHAW. Somewhere nice and quiet. Too much noise here. The animal spirits of the men . . .

INGLIS (*quietly*). Outrageous wee cunt.

SHAW. I can put it in writing if that would help speed up the process, Corp.

INGLIS. Trouble with you, Shaw, is underneath that lovely uniform . . .

SHAW. It's a bit of a doss-house without the cubicles, Corp.

INGLIS. . . . uniform, I've seen lads die in, yer still a fuckin crummy civvy. But don't worry, if I've got anything to do with it you'll get your bowler hat – just shortly.

Goes to his room and sits at his desk. Takes a bottle of whisky out and pours himself a glass.

UXBRIDGE (*in a low voice*). The way I see it, you owe me.

SHAW. Go away, little wasp.

UXBRIDGE. Doing fatigues when it's you who's screwed up.

SHAW. I suppose I am doing the instructors a favour. (*Giggles.*)

UXBRIDGE. Oh yeah?

SHAW. The secret of the uniform is to make a crowd solid. Collective punishment is part of the impersonal singleness of being a soldier. Part of your training, Uxbridge. You should thank me. I don't know why you grumble.

UXBRIDGE (*grabs him*). Don't know why I grumble? I'll tell you why. Cos I don't give a toss about being a bleeding soldier. Now, like I said, I reckon you owe me. So how's about a small donation?

SHAW. A donation? For what?

UXBRIDGE. Well, let's call it the Jack Uxbridge Ale Fund. What you say? You've got plenty. You'll have the satisfaction of knowing every penny will be lathered on drink – not a farthing wasted. (*They struggle.*) Just a pound. Just a pound. I've seen you buy as much grub for the lads in the canteen and not eat a crumb yourself. You're loaded.

UXBRIDGE *has him and forces* SHAW *to go into his pocket and produce some coins.*

That's it. That's it.

UXBRIDGE *is still holding* SHAW *when* BRUCE *enters with two mugs of tea.* UXBRIDGE *doesn't see him.*

Oh. We're two bob short.

BRUCE *grabs him from behind. The money spills onto the floor.* SHAW *picks it up as the two struggle. Suddenly* UXBRIDGE *produces a knife.* RUDE *enters with two mugs of tea.*

RUDE. Jesus shit.

BRUCE. Shut up.

RUDE. Want your tea, Uxbridge?

UXBRIDGE. In a mo.

RUDE. While it's hot?

UXBRIDGE. In a mo.

BRUCE *wraps a towel round his fist. Parries* UXBRIDGE's *first lunge and with the counter-punch floors him.* CORPORAL INGLIS *hears something and enters. His entry diffuses the situation.*

INGLIS. What's going on here?

BRUCE. Nothing, Corporal. Nothing at all. Uxbridge was . . .

RUDE. He was showing us a few steps of the Charleston. The Charleston.

UXBRIDGE. That's right. I slipped, didn't I?

INGLIS. This hut should have bars on aw the windows.

RUDE. Look, Corp. Look. (*He's doing a few dance steps.*)

INGLIS. To protect the sodding public. It's the fuckin London Zoo.

RUDE. Hey, Corp? Corporal Inglis. You're wanted at the Guard House. Sharpish. Sar' Major said to tell you, like.

INGLIS. Sar' Major? Right. (INGLIS *gets his bicycle.*) Inspection first thing, so attend to yer kit. It's no a picnic, nor a Shanghai Fanny Palace, Uxbridge. (*Exits.*)

BRUCE *goes to* UXBRIDGE *and helps him up from the ground.*

BRUCE. Pull a blade on me again and I'll take it off you and trim your lugs wi it.

UXBRIDGE. Yeah – alright.

BRUCE. Got a smoke?

UXBRIDGE. No.

BRUCE. Here.

UXBRIDGE. Ta.

BRUCE. A Shanghai Fanny Palace? He's a veteran right enough.

RUDE. Here's the mail, lads.

UXBRIDGE. Any for me?

RUDE. Hold your horses. Here we go. Rude. That's me. (RUDE *dispenses the letters onto a bed*). Shaw. Shaw. Shaw, Shaw. Bruce. Shaw, Shaw, Shaw.

BRUCE *collects the letters.*

How many wives you got, Shaw? Get a whiff of that?

BRUCE. How many folk meant to know you're here?

RUDE (*to* UXBRIDGE). Get a whiff of that.

UXBRIDGE. Lilac. Nice. She's keen.

RUDE. She's keen alright. Writes her letters naked. On the bed.

UXBRIDGE. That'll do. That'll do.

BRUCE. No one's meant to know.

RUDE (*reading his erotically charged letter*). Oh, for fuck sake. Oh, for fuck sake. She's in the kitchen making soup in the buff.

UXBRIDGE. Give the dog a bone. (*Pants like a dog.*)

BRUCE (*opens his letter*). It's from the Old Man.

> SHAW, *who hasn't bothered with his own letters, stops reading his book, and talks privately with* BRUCE.

SHAW. What does he say?

BRUCE. Hold on. He wants to know what likes your drill an bull. If you're keeping a journal.

SHAW. 'The garden, it was long and wide. And filled with great unconscious peace.'

BRUCE. Wants to know if you're attending church parade. If you're seeing anyone famous.

SHAW. Why is there no peace?

BRUCE. He says tae write back wi a full report. He's rented a cottage near the camp for you to go to when you need to write. Look.

SHAW. You know what that means? He will find fault. He wants to get rid of me. He will find fault.

BRUCE. Pull yourself together.

UXBRIDGE. What got him going?

BRUCE. Remember, you're a gent, sir.

SHAW. I am his puppet.

UXBRIDGE. Is he alright?

SHAW. I will endure. I must. Shan't I?

BRUCE. Why do you abide this dictator? It's full of insults. He calls you a . . . a Bastard.

SHAW. I'll write out this book. My bruised feet stagger forward on the road he has chosen for me.

BRUCE. I burn with shame to read the half of it. Says you're to be punished if you step out of line.

SHAW. It will not come to that.

BRUCE. This is gross, sir. We canny stop here.

SHAW. No. You are wrong. This makes me stronger.

BRUCE. Stronger? How?

SHAW. After I've paid in full, I will belong much more to myself. This serving in the ranks as a . . . as a . . . as a beast is the way it must be.

RUDE. Shaw, read this. Read it.

BRUCE. You can disappear. We can light out thegether. Say the word. We've lost him before.

SHAW. Not for very long. (*To* RUDE.) A woman?

BRUCE. Say the word.

RUDE. Too right. See what she says there. (*Gives him one page of his letter.*)

SHAW. Thank you, Rude.

BRUCE. What do we do? What do I write back?

SHAW. Put it away. We'll talk later. Now Rude. Which bit?

RUDE. That bit there. She's making pea broth in the buff. (SHAW *reads.*) Give Bruce a shot when you're finished.

BRUCE. I doubt I'm bothered.

UXBRIDGE. What about me?

RUDE. I'm off to find an empty stall. Anybody seen my spunk-rag?

SHAW. Uxbridge. (UXBRIDGE *takes the letter.*)

BRUCE. What do we do?

SHAW. I came here to eat dirt till it's normal. There's to be no peace. The Old Man will see to that. I am under his jurisdiction and must obey.

RUDE. Hey, somebody's blagged my spunk-rag.

UXBRIDGE. Rude, your woman is nude in this letter. All over the house starkers. Ho-ho.

RUDE. I can't find me spunk-rag. Come on, Uxbridge, give it back.

CORPORAL INGLIS *enters carrying a gramophone.*

UXBRIDGE. What the fuck?

INGLIS. Who in this hut do you think this music box belongs to? Who in this hut thinks the Tanks is a pink picnic party?

SHAW. Thank you, Corporal. I'll take charge.

BRUCE. We going to turn the hut into a dance hall?

UXBRIDGE. Yeah. You work the door, Jock. Keep the riffraff out. I never! (*Sings.*) 'Dear little girl, have I made you sad?'

RUDE. 'I'm sorry, dear, so sorry, dear.'

INGLIS. It's been stamped. Approved. Buggered if I know how.

RUDE. Mustard kit, Shaw.

INGLIS. Beyond the beyond. The Tanks is fucked.

RUDE. Does it work?

SHAW. We shall find out shortly.

UXBRIDGE. Oh no. I bet you anything you like it's fuckin that bleeding Mozart and and his bum-chum Beethoven. He's going to torture us with his bleeding posh tunes.

INGLIS. Clara Butt. She'd a pair of lungs. A nightingale.

SHAW. Chopin. We'll have Chopin with our supper, lads.

INGLIS. I heard her sing in 1915. Red Cross benefit concert. Nae playing after lights out or during Church Parade, Shaw. Nae vying wi the fuckin chaplain. Vicar thinks ragtime is music o the devil.

RUDE. On you go, Shaw. Crank her up.

SHAW. One moment.

RUDE. Chopin anything like Moonshine Kate?

UXBRIDGE. You wait, sonny. See if I'm right. Fuckin officer crap.

INGLIS. Army's getting too novel, too lax. Only music I heard during basic was wee Johnny Maglinchy and the whine o his pipes. Fuckin murder. Boche did for him in '18. Him and his pipes. 'Johnny, sac au dos.' That's French. Chopin's alright.

Music comes on. It's a comic song: Nellie Wallace, 'Always Blow the Candle Out'.

That's no Chopin.

RUDE. It's Nellie Wallace.

UXBRIDGE. Nice one, Shaw. Nice one.

RUDE. I love this one. 'Always look under the bed . . . '

INGLIS. Right . . . (*Takes the needle off the track.*) Inspection tomorrow, lads. Nice and sharp.

RUDE. Corp?

INGLIS. What?

RUDE. When do we get to drive a tank, Corp?

UXBRIDGE. Not on your nelly.

INGLIS. When we're all Chelsea Pensioners and safely out the road, son.

RUDE. When do we get to fire a decent bit of kit? A mortar even? No a pea-shooter.

INGLIS. Always remember, son, your standard tank barrage will put one round, just the one round, on the planned target just so, smack. That round will be a dud. Guaranteed. That's Inglis's law o combat no fuckin Marshal Foch.

UXBRIDGE *puts the record on again. The men join in the comic refrains.* SHAW *sits on his own in gloomy silence.*

Scene Six

Morning. Music changes . . . slowed down as it's been left on the gramophone too long. Another comic song: 'I must go home tonight, I must go home tonight, I don't care if it's snowing, blowing, I'm going. I only got married this morning, and it fills me with delight, I'll stay out next week as long as you like, but I must go home tonight.'

Lights up to empty barracks. CORPORAL INGLIS *in his room.* UXBRIDGE *and* RUDE *enter with towels, just back from the wash-house.* INGLIS *pours himself a whisky.*

RUDE. Bloody freezin.

UXBRIDGE. Well, you got a six-mile run to look forward to. That'll warm you. You ain't in charge of the fucking map, Rude?

RUDE. I didn't ask to.

UXBRIDGE. I ain't no tourist. I want back in time for dinner.

RUDE. Breakfast was slops.

UXBRIDGE. Did you try the black pudding?

RUDE. Like toffee it was. Cracked me tooth.

UXBRIDGE. Here. Where's Bruce and Shaw?

RUDE. Shaw's having his bath. Bath is his middle name. He pays that civvy-stoker Rodgers to have it hot first thing.

UXBRIDGE. Does he? He's not short of a bob.

RUDE. Hey, lovely job he done on that gun yesterday. Shell smack on the button.

UXBRIDGE. See the C.O. was spotted loitering with intent.

RUDE. Three thousand yards right down the hatch. That man can turn his hand to anything.

UXBRIDGE. Yeah, he got his rifle skills potting big game in Kenya. He's a show-off. Jock? Where's Jock?

RUDE. Scoffing the black puddings if he's not tossing his caber.

UXBRIDGE. Rude but probably true. (*He looks under* SHAW's *bed.*)

RUDE. What you doing?

UXBRIDGE. There's something fishy going on.

RUDE. Where?

UXBRIDGE. Where? Here in this fuckin billet. Him. He's a snoop.

RUDE. Who?

UXBRIDGE. Shaw. He's a spy.

RUDE. Is he?

UXBRIDGE. From up there.

RUDE. What? Up there.

UXBRIDGE. An officer, you tit. From the Ministry. You seen how the officers treat him with kid gloves.

RUDE. Get off it. Over-suspicious, you are.

UXBRIDGE. Even Inglis doesn't blow him out as much as you can tell he'd fancy to.

RUDE. He gave him push-ups yesterday for doing his back-chat in Latin.

UXBRIDGE. Never done scribbling. And all these letters he gets.

RUDE. He doesn't open half of them.

UXBRIDGE. See. Odd. Finding out who's who. What's what.

RUDE. He is a queer sort of bloke. But he's alright to me. Bought you a carton o Woodbines last week. Not shy to put his hand in his pocket. What you got against him?

UXBRIDGE. Here's one. Open it. (*Throws it to* RUDE.)

RUDE. I'm not. He's alright to me.

UXBRIDGE. Get on with it. He won't miss it. (UXBRIDGE *finds a letter* SHAW *is writing.*) Who's it from? Never mind reading it.

RUDE. Some geezer called George Bernard Shaw?

UXBRIDGE. I've heard of him.

RUDE. Maybe he's his dad.

UXBRIDGE. Let's see. (*Reading.*) 'With fond . . . ' Here, bet it's that young Brummie he keeps talking about. (*Mimicking* SHAW.) His Apollo with the oh-so-'vile' Brummie accent. It's a Molly name, i'nt it – Bernard?

RUDE. I don't want to read that.

UXBRIDGE. Watch out, then . . . Bingo.

RUDE. What?

UXBRIDGE. Watch that fuckin door. Shit. Oh, God strike me. God strike me.

RUDE. What? Read it out.

UXBRIDGE. You keep your eyes peeled. 'Today I washed up the dishes in the sergeants' mess. Messy feeders, sergeants: plates were all butter and tomato sauce, and the washing water was cold. I've been dustman and clerk and pig-sty cleaner.'

RUDE. Pig sty? What pig sty? We don't have pigs in the Tanks.

UXBRIDGE. He's referring to this hut, stupid. Keep looking. 'I've been housemaid and scullion. But the life isn't so bad.' The life isn't so bad.

RUDE. Well, that's true.

UXBRIDGE. You prick.

RUDE. Better than ploughing. Back-end of a shire horse all day.

UXBRIDGE. Do you know who this letter's addressed to, dipstick? You got any fuckin idea who he's writing to . . . ? (INGLIS *enters.*)

INGLIS. Who?

UXBRIDGE. Shit.

INGLIS. Who is it addressed to?

UXBRIDGE *hands it to* INGLIS.

You are a low-life. (*He reads it. Long pause.*) He calls him 'My dear . . . My dear Swanny.'

RUDE. Is that queer?

INGLIS. My dear Swanny. 'You asked for some details of my life here.'

UXBRIDGE. See?

RUDE. Who's Swanny?

UXBRIDGE. You tell him, Corp.

INGLIS. Only Air Vice-Marshall Sir Oliver Swann, laddie . . . R.A.F. Chief of Personnel and Training.

RUDE. Right. Is that queer?

UXBRIDGE. You dipstick.

INGLIS. You both keep your mouths shut. This goes no further. A man is not to be judged erroneously because he comes from a different sort.

UXBRIDGE. What's he doing here, Corp?

RUDE. He says he's a spy . . . from up there.

INGLIS. My Aunt Fanny's a spy tae, son. She's a spy for the pygmies. Oh aye. Reports directly to Emily Pankhurst. See, Pankhurst runs a secret cabal of blue-stocking midgets whose game is to get their paws on the secret levers of power that guide this blessed Empire of ours. They meet every Tuesday night under her petticoats. That's why women wear petticoats, laddie.

RUDE. Don't think so, Corp.

INGLIS. You fuckin twat. In my day this sort of thievery . . . stealing from a comrade, would earn you a midnight summons to the bath-house. The reception committee would be most unforgiving. Do you want your balls shaved in a tub of icy water? 'No' is the answer. Do you want to wander the land wi yer eyebrows shaved off completely? 'No' is the answer. Do you want a bath-brick shoved up your sorry arse? Do you want a leathering? What is the answer?

RUDE *and* UXBRIDGE. No, Corporal Inglis.

INGLIS. This place is a disgrace. (*Kicks over some stuff.*) Get it cleaned up. (*Exits.*)

UXBRIDGE. See? Who the fuck is he?

RUDE. He's a deep bastard.

UXBRIDGE. He's a deep bastard alright.

RUDE. Yeah, queer.

UXBRIDGE. You said it, mate.

INGLIS *in his room. Reads the letter. Opens the drawer in his desk. Takes out a half-bottle of whisky. Pours a large one. Downs it, crumples the letter slowly in his fist.*

Scene Seven

SHAW *is polishing his bike. The* M.O. *passes. The* M.O. *takes out his pipe. They engage in talk.*

M.O. Tinkering away, Shaw?

SHAW. Evening, sir.

M.O. I could never grasp the mechanical and such. Think the rain will hold off?

SHAW. I should think so, sir.

M.O. Forecast's stiff.

SHAW. Weather boys are always getting it wrong, sir – wind's in the east, sir.

M.O. It's not? Is it? A fine machine.

SHAW. A real flyer.

M.O. What type is she?

SHAW. The Brough Superior.

M.O. Brough Superior.

SHAW. The latest model, sir. Do watch the oil there, sir.

M.O. Sorry.

SHAW. Speed is my fix, sir.

M.O. I know. You passed me yesterday on the Bovington Road.

SHAW. I wasn't racing, sir. It's just I dislike other people's dust.

M.O. Indeed. Well, I got a bucketful of yours.

SHAW. It's my one luxury.

M.O. Motoring Alice into town, when you . . .

SHAW. Don't you think it's an instinct, sir?

M.O. An instinct? What is?

SHAW. The need to go fast.

M.O. An instinct?

SHAW. I've seen men beggar themselves for a fast horse. When my nerves get jaded. When my head turns to 'mind suicide'.

M.O. Now look here, Shaw.

SHAW. I'm terribly sorry, sir.

M.O. That kind of language won't do.

SHAW. I'm afraid I'm an incorrigible phraser.

M.O. Yes. Well. That sort of phrasing . . . is best left to novelists. Your are a pen man, I suppose. What were we talking about?

SHAW. Speed.

M.O. Motorbike – yes.

SHAW. Speed and its rewards.

M.O. The Brough Superior.

SHAW. I open up and I feel the earth under me comes alive. Everything blurs. All detail goes blank. Speed narrows everything down, like plunging into a white mist. Leaving everything behind in a fume of petrol. It's a craving. I could go on for hours about speed.

M.O. How fast do you push her?

SHAW. Eighty – ninety. Night-riding's best. No traffic to worry about. Nothing's on the roads after one.

M.O. Still. A dangerous hobby.

SHAW. Yes, risking everything for two and nine a day. But you've got to let a machine like this out full throttle. Keeps the two of us from getting sluggish.

M.O. She's your bus. Isn't that what they say? Your 'bus'.

SHAW. Boanerges, I call him.

M.O. Ah. A hero from old Homer?

SHAW. Nearly right, sir. It's a Greek compound – Boanerges: 'He who stirs up the war-cry.' A proper Thunderer. Unlike some.

M.O. (*irked*). Unlike some? How often does that mask of mildness float you clear of trouble, Shaw?

SHAW. I don't know to what you refer, sir.

M.O. I think you do. Act of stupidity may be necessary in your current company but it doesn't pull the wool over my eyes. I can't understand your attitude at all.

SHAW. Sorry if a mere nothing in uniform causes you alarm, sir.

M.O. No gentleman, sir, allows his passions to foul a calm understanding.

SHAW. I feel a good laugh works to enlarge the understanding much more than any education affluence bestows.

M.O. A man's character . . .

SHAW. Arabia rid me of my English 'character', sir. For which I'm grateful. Allows me to see and feel in a different light. You should try the desert. It has broad horizons, sir. Anyhow, that's how I found it.

M.O. A gentleman is not just someone who smokes a pipe as opposed to Woodbines. He is a man constant in his dealings. He does not play games with his station. It's simply not straight. It's akin to trickery at cards and such. Nor do I hold to the notion that there are some men on which one should suspend all judgment. Speaking candidly, sir, you sound a chap versed in 'cunning and hypocrisy' rather than any virtue. Speaking candidly.

SHAW. When virtue sleeps it awakens with improved vigour.

M.O. Do not bandy epigrams with me . . . sir. It all smacks of vanity. A monstrous overestimation. Yes, courage, in emergency . . .

SHAW. I was never brave, sir.

M.O. But self-mastery is blackguard if all it serves, by any means, is to augment belief in its own power. It matters not, if a little dust and dirt attend the matter. It is not edifying.

SHAW. In Damascus I was tyrant for a day and felt, sir, in my blood the relish of putting a man to the wall. I trod under boot the flesh of dying Turks. The dead and writhing material of history. My throne wasn't made of lentils, it was made of skulls. What medal do you think I deserve?

M.O. You're not a saint, damned it.

SHAW. I mean only to be my own judge, sir.

M.O. They were turbulent times for all. The war daubed us all in grime. Can you guess what is likely to befall a man who takes exaggerated moral responsibility for the wrongs of a whole political, social disaster?

SHAW. And it is not my place to assume responsibility, is it, sir? No one's place. All one can do is refuse reward for being a successful trickster. The best never came back, did they, sir? Oh, they did their best. Not their fault it was such a rotten best.

M.O. I should tell you I've talked . . . talked with the C.O. and your credit is running out. This game of yours is nearly over. Your friends in high places . . .

SHAW (*holds out his hand, palm-side up*). It's starting to rain, sir. Looks like the weather boys got it right. Better get under cover, sir.

M.O. I don't understand you . . . I simply . . .

SHAW. I don't care to be understood, sir. I won't be levelled down.

M.O. You look to me like a man, a man who's tumbled out of the bally future. Half-made and half-barking mad. (*Salutes.*) Good-day, Colonel Lawrence.

SHAW *does not return the salute.*

SHAW. Private Shaw, sir.

M.O. Oh, humbug, sir. Cant and quackery, sir. (*Rains. Exits.*)

SHAW *returns to cleaning his bike and giggles.*

Scene Eight

Music: 'Sheik of Araby.' Slows down. A hillside. Enter BRUCE *in his P.T. gear, carrying his rifle, followed by* UXBRIDGE *and* RUDE *in the same gear.*

BRUCE. No far now. No far. I can see the halfway marker.

UXBRIDGE. My legs are dead. They're dead.

BRUCE. Take deep breaths. Get the air back into yer . . . lungs.

UXBRIDGE. Tell you what. Time I'm finished this basic . . . no copper . . . no copper will ever catch me again. They'll need to put whippets in uniform.

RUDE. I had eggs this morning. India rubber eggs. They're still lying there . . . in the pit of me stomach.

BRUCE. Get your breaths steady. That's it.

UXBRIDGE. You'll make P.T.I. one day, Jock.

BRUCE. I did boxing.

UXBRIDGE. I knew you has.

BRUCE. I know how to train.

UXBRIDGE. Crisp as you like, over the top.

BRUCE. Where's Shaw? He was just behind us. Where is he?

UXBRIDGE. What is it with you two? Eh. What is it?

BRUCE. Never you mind.

RUDE. He's gone . . . sightseeing.

UXBRIDGE. It's like private bleeding Shaw's got himself an orderly. You're the only one seen the inside of that shack he sneaks off to. What you two do there?

BRUCE. He writes. I sit and watch him.

UXBRIDGE. Much he paying you? Come on, must be paying you something? What little racket you got going with him? Let us all in on it.

BRUCE. I've known him for ages. He's a friend. As good as.

UXBRIDGE. Who is he? Who is Shaw really?

BRUCE. Can't say.

UXBRIDGE. Come on, we're pals as well. As good as him.

BRUCE. I can't say.

UXBRIDGE. Only we don't pay you for our comradeship.

BRUCE. I've sworn it.

UXBRIDGE. He's a little toff getting his rocks off slumming it with the great unwashed. He thinks Tanks is Thomas Cook's.

RUDE. His middle name might as well be soap suds.

UXBRIDGE. What are you on about now?

RUDE. His baths. His morning scrubs.

BRUCE. There's things happening in this country you know nothing about. Forces underneath.

UXBRIDGE. What? Cloak-and-dagger fancy stuff, is it? He a red? A strike organiser?

RUDE (*sings*). 'We're all out for higher wages, / We're all out for better pay. / We'll never be content / Till we get the ten per cent / For we've a right to live as well as you.'

BRUCE. Unions are amateurs. Puppets.

UXBRIDGE. That so, Lloyd Jock.

BRUCE. I'll tell you what. I was wi Shaw in Soho, about two months ago, we were living rough, doss-house to doss-house, said he was being tailed. I didn't believe him. I never saw anyone. Then in the street, Soho, I was right beside him, he was shot at.

UXBRIDGE. You what? Shot at?

BRUCE. No jest.

UXBRIDGE. Shot at?

BRUCE. Aye, shot at. A motor – the other side of the street pulls up. The place is mobbed. This bloke leans out the window wi this huge fuckin Webley and fires two shots at us . . . at him. Bam! Bam! I seen him. Bullets smashes up shop window. I gets him down a side street. Motors tae Brighton that afternoon. Me in the side car. Spent weeks travelling the country – moving only at night. It was like he was just keeping one step ahead of them. We'd sleep rough or keep tae ourselves in digs. One of us always keeping watch over the other. He found something out, see.

UXBRIDGE. You're bein set up, Jock.

BRUCE. What do you know?

UXBRIDGE. You're just a young bloke, you know nothing.

BRUCE. An you're an ex-con.

UXBRIDGE. How do you know you're not being set up?

BRUCE. Who by?

UXBRIDGE. Who by? Who you think? By him. By fucking him.

BRUCE. Naw. You don't know him. I've spent time with him.

UXBRIDGE. And I've done time.

BRUCE. Met his friends. Seen the quality types he keeps. Been left alone in his house.

UXBRIDGE. What like's his patter? Con man always uses the same spiel. What like's his patter?

BRUCE. What's in it for him? (*Points to himself.*) . . . God, you're sly, Uxbridge. You're really sly. You just want to stick your scythe in someone else's corn. You nearly had me.

UXBRIDGE. Yeah, he picked you well, mate. That he did.

RUDE. Look out. Here comes bastard Inglis.

INGLIS *enters on his push bike.*

On his Brough, on his Brough Inferior.

UXBRIDGE. On his Brough Inferior. Good one, Rude. Like it. (*Laughing.*)

INGLIS. You lot stop for a brew-up? It heartens me to see you all having such a nice outing. What's so funny?

BRUCE (*dryly, referring to his laughing mates*). Sorry, Corp. It's the sight of you on yer Brough Inferior.

INGLIS. Oh, a wee joke from the Aberdeen loon there. Round of applause. You fish-person. You haddock-shagger.

BRUCE. That's Peterhead you're talking about, Corp. No us. We're sheep-shaggers.

INGLIS. I stand corrected. Sheep-shagger. Look at Uxbridge. He's off on one. Help steady him, Rude. Uxbridge, what gem o a remark are you wetting yourself to share wi us? Spit it out, laddie. I do so look forward to his verbal squibs. His verbal in general being jollity itself. Isn't that right, son?

UXBRIDGE. I was just wondering, Corp . . . just wondering how you works the throttle on your bike? On your Brough Inferior.

INGLIS. Oh, very funny. Do you mind if I nick that line for the N.C.O.s' mess? (INGLIS *punches* UXBRIDGE *very hard in the stomach.*) It being such a rib-tickler. I daren't tell my old mum that one – she'll spit her false teeth out into the fire. Haemorrhages all round the single-end. Not a dry seat left in the house. Talking of rib-ticklers an gags an such, where's Shaw?

RUDE. He took a detour, Corp.

INGLIS. What? A short cut?

RUDE. A detour, he said. Shaw said.

INGLIS *grabs him by the throat.*

Up to the ruins on Castle Hill, sightseeing. Don't hit me.

INGLIS. You better not have lost him. He better not come to any harm for your sakes.

RUDE. Says he's going to do all of today on a single choc bar, Corp. How can a man go as he goes without his dinner? He does it time and again.

INGLIS. He'll do it on a walnut if I had him.

BRUCE. I've seen him go on less, Corporal. I seen him go on air. Pure fresh air.

INGLIS. Aye. You could all do wi a lesson from him. There is much to admire in that wee toff. The smartness with which he volunteers for any shite detail has greatly impressed me of late. Always first to step onto the square. Shaw's got spine. First I thought, here's facetious, but naw, he's proved he's constant and it dissny bother him tae get stuck in. Look at the way he handles a gun. Idolise his kit. Idolise it. Fuck. What am I doing? I'm not going to talk to you lot about the nobility – honour – of being a soldier.

UXBRIDGE. You bastard.

INGLIS. Get that crap-hat doon the hill, out of my sight. You've got twenty-five minutes to get back to camp. Or I'll have you for AWOL. You don't want to end up in the pokey.

INGLIS *exits on his push bike.*

UXBRIDGE (*lifts his rifle, aiming after* INGLIS). I'd like to give him one. I'd like to pop that bastard.

BRUCE. Wouldn't we all?

UXBRIDGE *takes an illicit bullet from his shorts pocket and loads it into the chamber, snapping shut the bolt. Takes aim.*

Don't be daft. You fuckin mad? He's broken you if you do.

UXBRIDGE. His fuckin likes.

BRUCE. You want Inglis to win?

UXBRIDGE. How they gonna know who shot him?

BRUCE. They can tell.

RUDE. John's right, Jack.

BRUCE. Don't worry – his time will come.

UXBRIDGE. His likes.

BRUCE. His time will fuckin come.

UXBRIDGE. Got your word on that?

BRUCE. Promise. (BRUCE *takes the rifle, unloads it, puts the bullet in his pocket.*) 'Mon.

UXBRIDGE. OK. Got your word on it?

BRUCE. Cross my heart. Let's go. Halfway mark's over by. (*Exits.*)

RUDE. Dinner's out in an hour.

UXBRIDGE. Is it?

RUDE. It's Wednesday. You can have my bread pudding, Jack.

UXBRIDGE. Ta. Get going. I said fucking scram!

RUDE *exits.* UXBRIDGE, *looking back to where* INGLIS *has exited, takes a bullet out and loads it into the chamber.*

Scene Nine

SHAW, *in his P.T. gear, rifle slung across his back, climbs up to a perch on the castle ruins. Sits, cross-legged in silent meditation.* INGLIS *enters, pushing his bike.*

INGLIS. Are you alright? Shaw? Up there?

SHAW. Yes, Corporal.

INGLIS. What you doing?

SHAW. Sitting in silence. I like so much the being alone.

INGLIS. You've got a run to finish.

SHAW. You don't say.

INGLIS. A time to beat, Shaw. You're well behind.

SHAW. I couldn't resist. Castles are a thing with me. (*Makes to rise*.) I'll get on, Corp.

INGLIS. No, don't bother. It's alright. Take your time. Resume yer perch for God's sake. I'm having a fag. (INGLIS *lights up*.) Do you know this heap's history, then? What family-run extortion racket was headquartered here?

SHAW. No. No, how it works to repel attackers . . . that's what interests me. What was in the mind of its designer and whether he succeeded in his vision.

INGLIS. Not much to see.

SHAW. You'd be surprised how much the trained eye can spy. The gate is almost a castle in itself.

INGLIS. You're qualified . . . qualified in castles, then?

SHAW. Sort of. I was an archaeologist before the war. There isn't a Crusader Castle in the Lebanon or Syria I haven't tramped round. Or France. I suppose castles and how they're built has been with me since an infant.

INGLIS. Near East. Palestine and that. The war out there was a donkey ride along Blackpool beach. It was. Nice sunshine weather, know what I mean? A picnic compared wi France. Would you not say so, Shaw?

SHAW. Oh yes. Yes, a breeze.

INGLIS. Different from the old trench ding-dong.

SHAW. Yes, bit of a side-show.

INGLIS. That's what I've always said. A fuckin side-show.

SHAW. Suez . . . the oil – not very important. That's why we have a garrison of 80,000 in Mesopotamia this very day. I wrote a letter to *The Times*.

INGLIS. You like your letters. How's your book coming on?

SHAW. Fine.

INGLIS. You intend to publish?

SHAW. It's not for a popular audience.

INGLIS. You should have been in the Somme – the Somme. I say that word and through the soles of my boots I swear I can feel a little tremble o the ground. Just a little tremble. Barrage seeps right inside you, know what I mean?

SHAW. I understand from the chaps you're a veteran, Corporal.

INGLIS. Aye. Somme hardened us. We lost so many good lads. It made us grim, tough.

SHAW. It made the British army.

INGLIS. Battalion wit said we were quality not quantity. (*Laughs.*) Battalion wit said we had constitution like no Yank ever had. We had the Somme in our guts. I'll tell you about Battle of Combrée some day.

SHAW. And I shall describe to you the Wadi Rum.

INGLIS. Is that name o a battle?

SHAW. No. Perhaps a cosmic one though.

INGLIS. So what is it, then?

SHAW. Only one of the most spectacular sights in the whole of Arabia. A labyrinth of red sandstone, of vast boulevards, scrolled and twisted by wind and salt into shapes so strange it's perilous to the imagination. Sun like shards of glass, not dancing sunbeams like here in England.

INGLIS. I prefer green – I can't stand heat. My mum was a redhead.

SHAW. In the Wadi Rum, flesh ferments . . . I stopped there once, exhaustion. Lay in a little sand-grave to try and sleep. It was like lying in a white sarcophagus in the heart of the sun.

INGLIS. A golf course, see a golf course – noo, that is my ideal bit of turf.

SHAW. Did your war leave many scars, Corporal?

INGLIS. I got made up to a lieutenant. In charge of ma own squad of tanks.

SHAW. You were an officer.

INGLIS. Ay.

SHAW. That's interesting.

INGLIS. Losses so chronic in '18 – call for officers was made.

SHAW. Yes, I hear a lot of rankers used it as a means of getting out of the line.

INGLIS. Yes, that's right, some poor material. Men could hardly read a map. Let alone dish out orders.

SHAW. They scraped the bottom of the barrel.

INGLIS. They scraped the bottom of the barrel alright.

SHAW. The backside of humanity in officer's uniform. Must have been quite a sight.

INGLIS. I seen some right arses in officer school alright, Shaw.

SHAW. The steerage class of men fit only for stable duties . . . paraded as officers. Stomach-turning.

INGLIS. Yeah. That's right.

SHAW. Such men can never hold the larger political picture in their heads.

INGLIS. You not think so?

SHAW. They lack imagination. Inarticulate, but wonderful chaps really when you realise they could not have had the motive or the vision which sustains a genuine officer.

INGLIS. Here. Have you ever wondered why all battles get fought at the very junction of two or more map sheets . . . printed at different scales? You ever notice that?

SHAW. Yes. Very farcical. War is a chaotic misery. I mean, I think it must be.

INGLIS. Yes, it is. I must say. If you don't mind?

SHAW. Keeping one's sanity, one's head must be tricky.

INGLIS. If you don't mind me saying so.

SHAW. Carry on, Corporal.

INGLIS. I do think you did some wonderful things.

SHAW. Did I? Where?

INGLIS. Out there. Near East. Don't worry, mum's the word. Discretion.

SHAW. Officer to officer, eh?

INGLIS. That's it, sir. Yes, what you did deserves a chest full o
medals.

SHAW. Corporal Inglis?

INGLIS. Yes.

SHAW. I detoured here to search in these ruins. I don't know what
for. I inquired of a ruin, its oracle you might say. I shouted down
into its fucking well but the ruin never spoke back to me. I was
inquiring of my fate. Yes – and the ruin is closed. Today the
information desk is closed.

INGLIS. No need to be so sharpish, sir. I was just saying how I
admire . . .

SHAW. Inglis, there are fleas of all grades and it makes me feel
very awkward to have smaller creatures than myself admiring
me.

INGLIS. You're a bleeding oracle alright, sir.

SHAW. My name is Shaw. Private Shaw.

INGLIS. And I ain't no flea, sir.

SHAW. You'll oblige me if you can try to remember that.

INGLIS. I shall be happy to oblige you. Very happy. Shaw.

SHAW. Thank you, Corporal. It's all I ask.

INGLIS. Down that hill, Shaw. At the gallop. Come on. Let's be
having you. Broke your mother's heart but you'll no break mine.
Inconsequential little has-been. I'm nae fuckin flea. I was an
officer. Aye. Me wi pips. That made you laugh. Inglis, he's the
bottom of the barrel. Good for dirty work but not to be trusted
wi the mess etiquette. Detrimental to good order having me
calling out toast to the crown. Incapable of passing the port
the right way round the fucking table. Know what they did,
Shaw, know what they did two days after they took back my
commission? They had me doing orderly duties in their officers'
mess. Just to make a point. Ladling soup intae the regimental
silver. I should have poured it o'er their effing heads. I should
have asked: 'Hands up which o you fannies wants extras?'
Shower o toffee-nosed pricks. But I didn't. (SHAW *exits.*) I
didn't . . . did I?

Scene Ten

The barracks at night. The men listening to music. SHAW *reads a letter he has just finished writing.*

SHAW. Dear Robert, please do not accuse me of believing in nothing. And being too pure with it. It seems being right for most people is a species of self-preservation. I seem to have gone past the desire to know whether I am right or wrong. The self against self-preservation stage. This is a road I'm on and, looking back, there seems to be no possibility of me having chosen any other. You think I've finally fallen into a nihilism which cannot find even a false god to believe in. You're wrong. As a poet you tinker with words and what's real about them. You talk in the language of choice. I in another language altogether. My destiny? I flee towards it on my Brough. My head haloed in a blank white light. But I'm knuckling down to ordinary. We finish basic training next week. The square-bashing over. The men, I feel, now accept me. There is something here which under all the grime pleases me. Something unexceptional. Please burn these letters. I beg you to burn them all. P.S. The book is nearly there. The cottage is a god-send. No irony intended. Love to all. Hoots.

End of Act One.

ACT TWO

Scene Eleven

The barracks. Evening. Music's on low: 'I've Seen the Lights of Gay Broadway.' Men with their mugs of tea. Relaxed. Stand Easy. SHAW is sitting on RUDE's bed sharing a joke with him and UXBRIDGE. RUDE is wearing SHAW's motorbike goggles. BRUCE is off at the canteen.

RUDE. So . . . the chap said . . . his opinion was . . . Listen up. It's very funny.

SHAW. The chap said . . .

UXBRIDGE. He said you had a face like a camel. To be blunt, that's what he said.

SHAW. . . . how long contact with camels had affected my face.

RUDE. Out east?

SHAW. But I explained that it wasn't my face that had been in contact with camels.

RUDE *laughs.*

UXBRIDGE. I don't get it.

RUDE. You don't get it?

UXBRIDGE. Sorry. You need a punch line that mentions the derriere. At the very least.

RUDE. I've got a joke. Ask me for a match, Jack? Watch this, Shaw. (*Holding his cigarette.*) Ask me for a match.

UXBRIDGE. Here we go. Rude, do you have a match?

RUDE. Yes. My face and your arse. No, no.

SHAW *laughs.*

UXBRIDGE. Don't encourage him.

RUDE. My face . . .

UXBRIDGE. You're back to front, dipstick.

SHAW. It's the wrong way round.

RUDE. . . . . an your rump? Should be my arse and your face. Shit.

UXBRIDGE. And you think they're going to let you drive a tank. No chance. Here I've got a camel joke. And it ain't that Humphrey stinker. What do you call a camel?

SHAW. Humph-rey. Ho-ho.

RUDE. Go on, then.

UXBRIDGE. You ready for this, Shaw?

SHAW. I've a sinking feeling this won't be quite my flavour.

UXBRIDGE. This Captain transferred to a desert fort? Right? This Captain. A Frog Captain. Well, on his first inspection he spies a knackered old camel tied out the back of the enlisted men's hut. He asks the Sergeant, 'What's that camel for?' Sarge says, 'Well, sir, it's the middle of nowhere, and the men have natural urges, know what I'm saying, so when they get randy, we have the camel handy.' The Captain says, 'Well, if it's good for morale, it's alright with me.'

RUDE. Very funny.

UXBRIDGE. I haven't finished yet. After he's been at the fort six months, the Captain can't stand it no more, tearing his beard out, desperate he is, so he shouts to the Sarge: 'BRING IN THE CAMEL!'

RUDE. Bring in the camel.

UXBRIDGE. The Sarge shrugs his shoulders, as the frogs do, and leads the camel into the Captain's quarters. The Captain gets a foot stool out and well he gives it one, sharpish. He's going hell for leather. Giving it one. As he stepped down from the stool, well satisfied, buttoning his pants up, he asks the Sarge: 'Is that how, is that how, the enlisted men do it, Sergeant?' Sarge says, 'Well, sir, they usually just use the camel to ride into town.'

UXBRIDGE *laughs.* RUDE *looks perplexed.*

Where the cancan girls are in their silk stockings. Get it?

RUDE. I don't – no.

UXBRIDGE. Well, I'm not going to explain. I'll be here all night doing me copy of a jockey.

RUDE. I missed the bus on that one. Did you get it, Shaw?

SHAW. All too plainly.

RUDE. He never laughed.

UXBRIDGE. Bit too many bodily functions in it for him. You itching for a bath, Shaw? Too filthy, my wit?

SHAW. Very childish.

UXBRIDGE (*talking posh*). Tell me, old bean . . .

SHAW. Very silly.

UXBRIDGE. . . . do you find Bath a very clean city? So out east, Shaw, you went about by camel?

SHAW. Uxbridge, you are a noisy little sparrow . . .

UXBRIDGE. That must have been fun. Shag any?

SHAW. . . . caught in a lime trap – flapping away.

UXBRIDGE. I ain't snared . . . I'll work my passage clear. (*Plays a few notes on the mouth organ.*) Soon as it suits me.

SHAW. Nailed to a place against your nature.

UXBRIDGE. Maybe I should go with the flow and fade to a nothing. Like you. I've never seen your type before. A man volunteering for jankers.

SHAW. There are pleasures in commanding and in obeying. In command when it is not yet a habit and in obedience when it has become a habit.

UXBRIDGE. Bleeding hell. You do so like being deep. The man can't be weighed up. I've got spare ears for all your patter.

RUDE. Where you garage the bike then when you were out east, Shaw?

SHAW. In the garage.

UXBRIDGE. Here, where's Bruce got with the cake? My tea's getting cold. God, what I'd do for a pint of stingo. Talking of camels, I was on a donkey once. Scarborough beach. The penny ride. I was only nine. I'm on the back of this donkey and I gets it into my head to steal it. What was I going to do with it? Flog it round the doors? Anyway, I digs my heels in and the donkey takes off at a right healthy trot. Right along the beach. I looks back – the donkey men have got a posse out after me. A horde of them belting down the beach. That just spurs me on. I kicks it to a gallop. Time they got me, donkey had its tongue out – near to death he was. Frogmarched to the police station. What a leathering I got. One from the coppers and one from Dad. Mother always said that was the start of my misadventures. Long fingers I have. And proud of it. Why not? A man has to make his way in the world with what's given him . . . and what's not. Me and the law is naturally at odds. What you think of the law, Shaw? You know, bending it a bit? Shoving it where it belongs. I bet you have.

SHAW. There are too many honest men in the world – a few more rogues would make the world a much more interesting place, yes.

INGLIS *enters, in his army overcoat. He's been drinking.*

UXBRIDGE. And I mistook you for a gent.

INGLIS. You're not the only one – nae honour round here.

UXBRIDGE. If you insist, Corp.

SHAW. In Arab lands, a man's honour is the law.

INGLIS. 'The fear o hell's a hangman's whip to keep the wretch in order / But when you feel your honour slip let that aye be your border.' Burns. That's Robert Burns.

Exits into his room.

SHAW. Doesn't the oaf know the reward of honour and truth is invariably destruction?

UXBRIDGE. He's in a melancholy mood. Smells like a distillery. He'll be giving us it later, how he beat the Boche. Single-handed.

SHAW. Watch out for the surprise I've got for him.

UXBRIDGE. What surprise?

SHAW. Later. You'll see.

RUDE (*got his scrapbook out, doodling in it*). Shaw, what's your idea of a right good night out?

UXBRIDGE. He's teetotal – what would he know?

RUDE. I'm putting it in my scrapbook for Jill to read.

SHAW. A good night out? Let me think.

UXBRIDGE. Can such a number be pulled off sober? I pray not.

SHAW. I think, to take a chap out on the Brough. At speed.

UXBRIDGE. That's promising.

RUDE. On the Brough (*Writes*.) at speed.

SHAW. Go somewhere decent. Nice. A decent town. Give the chap a good feed. But that's OK up to a point. To make it a really excellent night I'd want my companion to be mildly a ruffian. I would study the man's peculiarities unseen. Watch how he conducts himself. Little or no talk. It's better that way.

UXBRIDGE. Bloke with gift of the gab is wasted on you.

RUDE. Take me on one of your night runs, Shaw?

SHAW. You just need to ask, Rude.

UXBRIDGE. What about me – down to The White Horse? That's all I ask.

SHAW. Not a problem, Jack.

UXBRIDGE. That's it, mate – you're generosity itself for a just cause, you are. Can I tap you for a pound?

SHAW. No. You've sponged all my savings this week. You are a mooching mendicant.

INGLIS *enters with the mail.*

INGLIS. I forgot. There's yer fuckin mail. (*Throws the bundle onto a bed and exits back into his office.*)

RUDE. Any for me?

UXBRIDGE. Give the dog a bone. Give the dog a bone.

RUDE. Shaw. Shaw. Shaw, Shaw, Shaw. Rude. Shit. It's from my bleeding mother.

UXBRIDGE. Oh. Is she a bit of alright? Let's see.

RUDE. Get your own bleeding mother. Shaw . . . Shaw. Bruce. Where's Bruce? Jock around?

SHAW *starts.*

UXBRIDGE. He's at the canteen. Give us it. I'll make sure he gets it.

RUDE. Shaw, Shaw. How many wives you got, Shaw? Hey, Corp is in a foul mood.

UXBRIDGE. Pissed in his pig's billet, as usual.

RUDE. Very maudlin mood he's in.

UXBRIDGE. The weeping veteran routine.

RUDE. He'll get a rocket, he will. Sooner or later. Like nobody's business. Right up his cunt-guts.

UXBRIDGE. With any luck, it'll be me who gives him it.

RUDE. It's a lofty letter Jock's got. Look, copperplate, not rough written. He doesn't usually get any.

UXBRIDGE. Not that I've noticed. Let's hide it from him.

SHAW. No.

UXBRIDGE. Has it got a whiff of girl? Smell it.

RUDE. Smells of . . . starch. Starch. Yeah. Starched cuffs an collars.

UXBRIDGE. Must be official. Sounds like a lawyer. Ain't you going to open your letters, Shaw? Entertain us, come on. I like the way they big shot's put it. All peacock an gobstoppers. La-di-dah. Go'n, give us some of your toffology.

SHAW. The air in here's a little hot. (*Drinks from his canteen.*)

RUDE. OK, Shaw. For the album. Favourite colour's what?

SHAW. It's an oven in here.

RUDE. Favourite colour?

SHAW. Scarlet.

UXBRIDGE. The scarlet pimpernel. See.

RUDE. Favourite dish?

SHAW. Bread and water.

RUDE. Favourite musician?

SHAW. Mozart.

UXBRIDGE. What rot. I'd rather listen to the chaplain spouting.

RUDE. Favourite character in history?

SHAW (*thinks*). Nil.

RUDE. Greatest pleasure?

UXBRIDGE. Nil? What about Napoleon?

SHAW. He was a vulgar genius – everything he did was to please the crowd.

RUDE. Greatest pleasure?

SHAW. Sleep.

RUDE. Greatest pain?

SHAW. Can't you guess –

UXBRIDGE. Put down 'noise'.

RUDE. Greatest fear?

SHAW. Animal spirits.

UXBRIDGE. Can I borrow your spunk-rag, Rude?

RUDE. Shut it. Greatest wish, Shaw?

SHAW. To be forgotten by my friends.

UXBRIDGE. You best stop writing letters to all and sundry, then.

RUDE. To be forgotten by my . . . pals.

UXBRIDGE. Getting like a sorting office. I fancy a letter. Someone to take an interest. Some girl. Some girl I met in the park or somewhere. That would do. A lady's maid. Smart. With thin ankles. A bit of manners. Not a surly barmaid-type too able to hold her ground with roughs or an old piano singer with fag smoke blown down her nostrils and licking her lips cos you slung her the bone of a compliment. 'Hello darling. What you fancy, honey?' But a proper girl. She can believe in God all she wants. Breezy and with a laugh clear as glass. Whose cunt is still a sacred mystery and not the bleedin tunnel of love for half the Navy. Do such girls exist? I've spied them coming out typing school, on the station platform. It must be dandy to have principles. God, principles must make seducing a virgin real fun. I've been in love. I have. My heart isn't made of tar. It still sweats a little. I fucked it up by being gallant. I'm not talking manners. Just that picture palace crap. Still might happen. Some decent girl give me the glad eye on the omnibus. I ain't bad lookin. God, what I'd give for a pair of tits to sink me face into. Swear it. To just bawl tears into a woman's big soft jugs. That'd do. But everything's fucked up. Everything's scabbed over. My prospects are same as a chimney sweep for eating ashes. Dead cert. Maybe you're only meant to see something beautiful just the once . . . just the once in your miserable life. My life is crap. That's what it is – crap.

SHAW. Everyone's life is disappointment.

UXBRIDGE. Is it? I don't think so.

RUDE. Nobody loses all the time, Jack.

INGLIS *enters.*

INGLIS. Have I . . . Have I ever told you lads about Combrée? Combrée in France? Have I never told you? Must have?

RUDE. Uh-oh. He's loaded.

UXBRIDGE. Do join us. Welcome. Welcome to the sunny half of the billet. We'd love to hear your story, Corp. (*Kicks* SHAW'*s bed.*) Wouldn't we, Shaw?

SHAW. Yes. Yes.

UXBRIDGE. Nice and cozy. Sit yourself down, Corp.

RUDE. All pals – muckers together. The way it should be. Shouldn't it?

SHAW. Nothing like the barrack-room communism to weld us all snug together.

INGLIS. Nae Bolsheviks in my hut. Mutiny and socialism go thegether. I won't fuckin have it.

RUDE. He didn't mean it that way, Corp.

INGLIS. Bolsheviks should be rounded up –

UXBRIDGE. Settle down.

INGLIS. Marched down nearest back street and knocked on the head.

UXBRIDGE. You know he can't help it. He can't resist a dig.

INGLIS. If I had my way – you'd have your bowler hat, Shaw.

SHAW. I apologise, Corp. Combrée. Battle of. Pray continue.

RUDE. Yes, Corp. Come on.

INGLIS. Combrée.

RUDE. Over by. In France.

INGLIS. Three hundred tanks.

RUDE. Three hundred. That first time tanks got proper usage?

INGLIS. Aye.

SHAW. Against the Hindenberg line. Wasn't it, Corporal?

INGLIS. Aye.

SHAW. Punched a nine-mile bulge behind enemy lines, Rude.

INGLIS. Aye.

UXBRIDGE. A riveting yarn so far, gents. I mean the to and fro.

RUDE. Was there a lot of mud, Corp? A lot of mud?

INGLIS. Mud to the right of us. Mud to the left of us. Mud all round.

UXBRIDGE. Lots of mud, then.

INGLIS. We crossed the Hindenberg line. Broke through their wire just before dawn. Down into the German back areas. Boy, were they surprised to see us over their baked beans. Couldny surrender fast enough. We thought, this is too easy. Usual rule is if your attack's going smooth, you've walked into an ambush, know what I mean? But no, it was just a very poor type of Boche that area. Small and unshaven. Dirty. A lot of them wearing spectacles. Cartoon Germans. We stopped for a fag, round up the prisoners . . . some of the men did a bit of looting. Then we pushed on. Pushed on. Two miles an hour maximum speed.

RUDE. Two miles an hour. That all? My old granny wi rickets can run faster than that.

INGLIS. Maximum. Then it started. Four tanks to ma right went up in flames. They'd found our weak spot. Get a man on top and a grenade down the hatch. Simple. I heard them clambering o'er our tank. The hatch opens, I looks up and there's a dirty great German . . . our mugs inches apart.

UXBRIDGE. Not a cartoon German either.

RUDE. You shot him?

INGLIS. I had my revolver oot.

RUDE. You shot?

INGLIS. But it was like my arm was paralysed. I couldny lift it.
We're face to face, see? I couldny lift my arm. Everything else
was workin.

RUDE. You could have stabbed him, Corp. Stab him in the face.

INGLIS. We're face to face . . . see.

UXBRIDGE. Could you smell his sausage breath?

RUDE. You kill him? You kill him? I would have.

UXBRIDGE. You think so?

INGLIS. I pished myself. That's what I did. I felt the liquid running
down my leg. It was his face. His face. Then Fritz's gone.

RUDE. He peed himself.

INGLIS. After that, time just stretched into one long . . . Brain
freezes. A man shows himself in battle. It's fuckin bedlam. All
I'm thinking is 'expend the amo'. Expend the amo. Use it up
and get the fuck out of here. Bullets are coming in through the
slits, pinging around the metal. Two of my men are hit. I get hit
myself in the chest. I want to lie down. There's nowhere you can
lie down in a tank.

UXBRIDGE. Funny time for a kip.

INGLIS. A 'sucking chest wound' is nature's way of telling you to
slow down, Uxbridge, know what I mean? Tank's full of smoke.
Tommy cookers, that's what our tanks were.

SHAW. It's too hot in here.

INGLIS. I bail out and run . . . stumble into a shell hole. Stinking
hole. Up to my waist in battle shit. I've got company. A dead
Hun. I'm sinking into the filth at the bottom o the hole. I get his
rifle, stick it into the wall as far as it will go. Lean on it. I hid
there until it's dark. Trying to get back out that hole was
something else. Mud like an octopus – no letting go. Climbing
out the mud sucked my boots off. Then I crawl back to our lines.

RUDE. Fuck sake, Corp. What happened to your crew?

INGLIS (*shrugs*). Put it this way, I never saw them again.

RUDE. You did what you had to do.

INGLIS. You're no listening, son. A man shows himself in battle.

RUDE. Your chest and that.

INGLIS. My chest?

UXBRIDGE. The sucking chest wound.

INGLIS. Naw. Naw. Shrapnel hit my watch. (*Pulls out his fob watch.*) Hit my watch, look.

UXBRIDGE *takes it.*

I had it in my shirt pocket. I never usually keep it there.

UXBRIDGE. It's got a dent in the case.

INGLIS. Must have been meant.

RUDE. I can't see anything.

INGLIS. We lost twenty thousand.

SHAW. I could never see any difference between victory and defeat.

RUDE. What, that? Must have been something else hit it. That's tiny.

Takes it and holds it up to look at it.

INGLIS. I'm telling you – it would have came out the back of me. It still works as well. Never misses a second.

RUDE *has managed to drop the watch into his mug of tea.*

My father's and afore him . . . his faither's. Give it me.

RUDE. Shit, Corp.

INGLIS. Give it me.

RUDE. Shit, Corp, I didn't mean it.

INGLIS. I know you didn't mean it.

RUDE. Sorry.

INGLIS. You're a dumb fuck, Rude. It's as simple as that. You are a menace. You will never make a bleeding trooper.

RUDE. Come on, Corp.

INGLIS. Who in their right mind would want to be in your team on the battlefield? Odd objects get shot at. And you are certifiably fuckin odd.

UXBRIDGE. Calm down, Corp.

INGLIS. Calm down? It's fuckin stopped. It's been through Ypres, the Somme. Couldny get past you. Been through mud an shit. You little . . .

UXBRIDGE. Shaw, tell him to calm down. Tell him.

SHAW. Corporal. Corporal Inglis. Why couldn't you kill that German. Why?

INGLIS. I don't know why.

SHAW. It's what happens when the joining-up spirit clashes with the human refusal to kill one of its own kind. It's stronger than you think. Stronger than *they* would have you believe.

INGLIS. You could have shot him, Shaw? (*Takes a swig of whisky from his mug.*) You could have plugged him.

UXBRIDGE. Could you?

INGLIS. Bet you could have shot him.

RUDE. Shaw would have plugged him.

INGLIS. Your hand wouldny have froze.

SHAW. Why are you still in uniform, Corporal? That's what I can't understand.

INGLIS. Flattest day of my life when the war ended. That's how.

SHAW. Now that I understand.

INGLIS. And it's a fuckin job – doubt you'll understand that one, Shaw. Civvy street doesn't give a toss for our sort.

BRUCE *enters with the cakes on a tray.*

BRUCE. Sorry, lads. A queue a mile long in the canteen.

RUDE. Oh, cheers, Shaw.

UXBRIDGE. Well done, Shaw. Can I?

SHAW. Muck in, lads, muck in.

BRUCE. Wire in, Corp. Have a wad.

INGLIS *looks round in disgust . . . goes back to his room. Drains the last of the whisky into his mug.*

What's up with him?

SHAW. Can't say.

UXBRIDGE. Here's your letter, Jock. Well, don't you want it?

BRUCE *takes it.* SHAW *shivers.*

Mmm. Cake's lovely.

BRUCE. It's from the Old Man.

SHAW. I know. What's the drill?

BRUCE. He wants you punished for 'gross indiscipline'.

SHAW. Punished.

BRUCE. Punished, it says here.

SHAW. Is that his sentence?

BRUCE. For not completing the manuscript to deadline.

SHAW. For all my freakish doings.

BRUCE. For chancing your life night-riding. For your fancy visitors.

SHAW. Where? When?

BRUCE. Tomorrow. At the cottage. Clouds.

SHAW. He has arranged everything it seems. Rude. (*Making sure* INGLIS *can hear.*) For the album. Would you like a list of my broken bones? My wounds.

RUDE. Your broken bones?

SHAW. And scars.

RUDE. Sounds good. You broke a few? I'll write them down.

SHAW. There's a bit of a heap, I'm afraid.

RUDE. Wait till I give me pencil a lick. Where'd you get them?

SHAW. Here and there. We'll start with the fractures first . . . write down fibula . . . then there's the radii, metatarsal, phalanges, costes, clauces . . .

RUDE. Stop. Stop. For God's sake, stop. For God's sake, how you spell . . .

A sudden crash, as INGLIS *has popped onto his bed and went right through as the slats have been removed from beneath his mattress.* UXBRIDGE *spits out his cake.* BRUCE *is left alone with the letter.*

UXBRIDGE. What was that?

INGLIS. Shaw! Shaw! You wee bastard!

RUDE, SHAW *and* UXBRIDGE *go to the door of* CORPORAL INGLIS*'s room, laughing.*

Scene Twelve

Night. The hut is in darkness. SHAW *has a fever.* BRUCE *is mopping his brow and helping him drink from his canteen. Everyone else is asleep.*

BRUCE. It's alright. Here, take these. (*Puts a pill in* SHAW*'s mouth.*) That's it. God, you're boiling. Got some of that desert sun inside you, eh?

SHAW. He will never let me rest.

BRUCE. Listen, he can be beat. The Old Man can be beat.

SHAW. No rest, no peace.

BRUCE. We can light out together.

SHAW. No escape. Water, please.

BRUCE. We can light out together. (*Gives him water from canteen. Checks other canteen, both are empty.*) I'm going to the bath house – get some water. Back in a tick.

SHAW. Water. Sand in my mouth. Sand.

BRUCE *exits. Flickering cinema images, half-seen, flood* SHAW*'s bed. He tosses and turns.*

Who is it? Who's there? Who's there?

LOWELL THOMAS *enters, smoking. Wearing a mac and fedora.*

THOMAS. It's me, Lawrence. (*Removes his hat.*) It's me.

SHAW. I refuse to be 'celluloided'.

THOMAS. Yes, you do so hate handing over editorial control to others. Why? When you are so adept at hiding in the spotlight.

SHAW. I refuse to be . . .

THOMAS. Was it worth it, Lawrence? The gift of freedom you tried to give those ungracious Arabs?

SHAW. Cut-throats. Cut-throats.

THOMAS. Yes. They have sunk back into their usual ways.

SHAW. Poor material. No stamina of mind.

THOMAS. Unlike you. You have lots of stamina of mind. Look at you. What are you doing in this hole?

SHAW. Dahoum.

THOMAS. You're way off the map. Terra incognita, old boy.

SHAW. Dahoum. Dahoum.

THOMAS. Ah, Dahoum.

SHAW. Lovely boy. Excellent material for improvement. He is coming with his donkey, water cans clanking.

THOMAS. I can hear him. In your head.

SHAW. He's laughing.

THOMAS. Dahoum is dead, Lawrence.

SHAW. Always laughing.

THOMAS. 1916. The war got him. Famine in Palestine.

SHAW. We wrestled in the sun.

THOMAS. You wrestled with The Bey.

SHAW. He is so small. Agile.

THOMAS. Excellent material for improvement.

SHAW. Wonderful summer . . .

THOMAS. 1911. Bathing in the sea.

SHAW. Blissful bathing in the sea . . . wonderful boy . . . nice savage. I wore his dishdasha . . . we swapped clothes . . . wore different worlds.

THOMAS. He thought the taps in England were works of magic.

SHAW. Water.

THOMAS. Wanted one to take home as a gift.

SHAW. Water . . . sand in my eyes.

THOMAS. They would have made him a sheik on the spot.

SHAW. I loved him.

THOMAS. You forgot him.

SHAW. 'I loved you, so I drew tides of men into my hands . . . '

THOMAS. Your unclean hands.

SHAW. I loved him.

THOMAS. You forgot him. How sad you are. Never mind. You have your various disguises to amuse you.

SHAW. Costs. Costs . . . It costs too much.

THOMAS. Like an actor in a foreign theatre, playing the part day and night for months without rest. Leave your English friends and customs on the coast.

SHAW. Leave them.

THOMAS. Come with me back to the Hejaz. Back to the Wadi Rum. Come with me, Lawrence.

SHAW. Wear Arab clothes.

THOMAS. Wear Arab things, go the whole way.

SHAW. The road is full of flints.

THOMAS. Never relax . . .

SHAW. Pebbles screaming in the sun.

THOMAS. . . . your watchful imitation.

SHAW. My white indoor skin . . .

THOMAS. Your mouth is full of sand.

SHAW. . . . Hurts . . . hurts . . .

THOMAS. Shall I describe The Bey's whip? Shall I? A thong of black hide, tapering from the thickness of a thumb down to a hard point finer than a pencil. The grip is engraved with silver.

SHAW. No, no.

THOMAS. A thong of black hide.

SHAW. Beginning and end of the secret . . . Beginning and end . . . of the secret . . .

THOMAS. What secret? What secret?

SHAW. . . . the secret of handling them . . .

THOMAS. Arabs?

SHAW. . . . is endless study of them. Keep always on your guard, never say anything unnecessary, watch yourself all the time. Hear all that passes, search out . . . search out what is going on under the surface, read their character, discover their tastes and weaknesses.

THOMAS. Keep everything you find out to yourself.

SHAW. Bury yourself in Arab, have no interests, no ideas except the work in hand, so brain is saturated with one thing only, and you realise your part so deeply so no little slips to counteract the painful work of months. Your success will be . . . will be . . .

THOMAS. Will be equal . . .

SHAW. . . . to the amount of mental toil devoted to it . . . to it.

THOMAS. Stamina of mind. Back to stamina of mind. Was it worth it, Lawrence?

SHAW. Water.

THOMAS. What a mess you British made.

SHAW. The heat hums.

THOMAS. You only got two things right about the Arabs.

SHAW. Dry as ashes.

THOMAS. The camels and the sand. That's about it . . . Remember when you blew the track at . . . at . . . I've completely forgotten. I've forgotten where. Does it matter? You blew up so many trains. Well, anyway, you pushed down the plunger and set your savages loose. A box car had fallen into a gully, tossed there like a toy by the explosion. You went and pulled aside the door. It was full of sick and wounded Turks. A stinking mass of tumbled soldiery. Do you remember? Peering into that ghastly typhoid darkness.

SHAW. Gasping like fish . . .

THOMAS. The box car was dripping blood. You thought it was oil.

SHAW. Gasping like fish . . .

THOMAS. Putrid fish . . . smelling wounds . . .

SHAW. Gasping, gasping.

THOMAS. Was it worth it, Lawrence?

SHAW. Get off. Get off.

THOMAS. I'm going. Don't worry. I know not to overstay my welcome.

SHAW. I refuse to be 'celluloided'.

THOMAS. Yes, you do so hate the editorial control being with others.

SHAW. Water, please.

THOMAS. Got some of that desert sun inside you, eh? What a lot of it there still is inside you. Sizzling away. (*He puts his hat back on.*) Tell me. The last time I saw you. In London. You were being tailed. Followed. That shadow. The one tailing you. Did it ever catch up with you? So long, until tomorrow.

Exits. BRUCE *enters with canteens full.*

SHAW. Water, water.

BRUCE. Here. I was thinking, we can light out together.

SHAW *drinks.*

SHAW. Tomorrow. Tomorrow.

BRUCE. Get a job on a boat. They're always recruiting. Stewards. You can do your book at night. It can't be worse than this. You'll be shot of the Old Man. What do yi say, eh? Eh?

SHAW. The Old Man. (*Giggles.*) Oh yes, the Old Man. Tomorrow, tomorrow we'll visit the ruins. Castellations. Castellations. In the Apulian-Romanesque manner. (*Giggles.*)

Scene Thirteen

Cloud Cottage. We see a desk with thick piles of paper. SHAW's *book,* Seven Pillars. *Lights from traffic flash past the cottage. We hear the sound of rain. The roar of a motorbike.* BRUCE *enters wearing goggles, he carries a long package.* SHAW *comes in after him. Pause.* SHAW *takes the package from* BRUCE.

SHAW. What's important . . . what's important is you note every detail. Every detail, understood?

BRUCE. Aye.

SHAW. In your report.

BRUCE. I know. You said.

SHAW. He looks for details.

BRUCE. Details, right.

SHAW. Write the letter tonight.

BRUCE. I've never been up tae this sort o thing . . . afore. I don't feel too good.

SHAW. Write while the details are fresh in your head. Clear this stuff away. (*Referring to the piles of paper.*) We'll use the table.

BRUCE (*picking up a sheet of paper*). It's coming . . . along?

SHAW. He levies every spare second. A treadmill, writing.

BRUCE. It's a right auld ocean o word, sir.

SHAW. Rewriting. He thinks my pen a gramophone needle, that this is a credible record of events. (*Giggles.*) They will read my penny-dreadful as an epic. That's the joke in writing one's own dispatches.

BRUCE. You mean it's all made up?

SHAW. Who can tell? Who can see at one and the same time through the veils of two customs, two educations, and not go a little bit off the rails? I remember many times my reason left me and outside myself . . . looked down on its trudging, mechanical body.

BRUCE. I'm not sure I can do this, sir.

SHAW. It has a purpose.

BRUCE. I'm not sure I can.

SHAW. My nerves get so overwrought, you see.

BRUCE. I don't know all these things.

SHAW. In Bedlam, beatings were rather like electric-shock therapy. A treatment for the nerves.

BRUCE. It goes against the grain wi me. It makes me feel. I don't know – stupid, actually. Like a mug. Kind o work hanger-ons do casual. It's no me. You pledged it wouldny come to this.

SHAW. I have tried to resist him. Believe me, I have begged for this not to happen . . .

BRUCE. Your friends – can they no help you?

SHAW. They can't be trusted. My friends, as you call them, would only help for personal gain. You do not know what is to be gained and won't be disappointed if you gain nothing.

BRUCE. Is that proper?

SHAW. Yes.

BRUCE. Why don't you use your name? Go to the papers.

SHAW. The press? Ha. I was a flash in the pan.

BRUCE. You are Lawrence, man.

SHAW. That's all done and dusted. I could never go to the press.
    What have I done anyway that's so astonishing?

BRUCE. You are Lawrence.

SHAW. And he was a filthy Empire trickster. Who was he? Where
    is he? Who is he?

BRUCE. I don't fuckin know.

SHAW. My guess is all the words of the yellow press, the whole
    alphabet of education were heaped up and juggled until he,
    Lawrence, stepped forward fully fated to utter each word
    and deed perfect. The mother tongue begets her crippled sons.
    I am a story within a story, there's no escape. I want my brain
    dead. This fable . . . (*Referring to the manuscript.*) a bastard's
    paper shit. Unclean, a mangy skin, stuffed and set up squarely
    for all men to gape at. That's their hero. Well, they can keep
    their rotting laurels. This my monument of scabs to this shitty
    little country and its filthy wars. Let the oafs salute away. My
    friends in the first rank of apes.

He takes a pistol from the desk drawer.

BRUCE. What's that in aid of?

SHAW. Everything is too ghastly for words.

BRUCE. I'm not going to wrestle you for it. Hand it to me.

SHAW. Better to die than go on living here.

BRUCE. Give me it. (*Knocks the gun out of* SHAW*'s hand.*) I need
    to meet the Old Man. I need to see him with my own eyes.

SHAW. You doubt his existence?

BRUCE. I don't know what to think.

SHAW. You think I lie?

BRUCE. No. Six months ago I was standing in a nightclub
    doorway, right? Blowing into my hands to keep the cold off.

Doesn't seem like such a bad number now, I can tell you. Dealing wi drunks. You could see what they were. Straightforward garrulous drunks . . .

SHAW. The remittance is not enough. Is that it?

BRUCE. The wages, the money's just fine – more than. I suppose I'm chafing. A loathe this army shit. Cooped up in this uniform. My folks urny for the army – never have been. I don't feel at liberty. And it's making me daft. Daft-like.

SHAW. We must carry out his orders.

BRUCE. You need to be free even to be remotely bothered. Noosed you don't see anything. Better if this was unforced . . . If it was unforced, then I'd see the life of it . . . of you, better.

SHAW. You shall meet the Old Man. It shall be arranged.

BRUCE. I know I'm a mere sparrow. To be associated wi . . . the like o yoursel . . . and the sorts you ken but . . .

SHAW. I trusted you to do this. I trust only you. I trust only you.

BRUCE. You trust no one?

SHAW. I've been sold out too often.

BRUCE. No faith like in no one else?

SHAW. There is no one else. None.

BRUCE. None to trust in the whole fuckin country? You?

SHAW. Impossible to trust.

BRUCE. No one?

SHAW *shakes his head.*

Very well I'll do it. (*Touches the birch.*) Shit sake. I think I need a fag, yi ken?

SHAW. Yes, have your cigarette.

BRUCE *lights up.*

BRUCE. I need to think. Ponder this.

SHAW *unbuttons his trousers.*

I need fresh air, ken. This is the ground-ebb. Tide doesny go oot any further than this. (*Exits.*)

SHAW. Yes, you must have a think. I am sorry.

SHAW lies belly down across the table. Braced almost as if he's riding his bike, leaning forward. Long pause. Traffic sounds.

Mud. Everything is mud. When will the curtain fall on this misery? A clock that's wound down – that's me. I favour a vehement displeasure to a feeble pleasure. A brutal agitation is all that rouses me. But I am not a brave man. 'The suspense is killing me. I hope it lasts.' (*Giggles.*) It is ever as the lady cried: 'The suspense is killing me. I hope it goes on and on and on.' I'll learn all pain . . . all pain until no longer actor but spectator . . . Not caring how my body squeals and jerks. (*Long pause.*) My dear Swanny. My dear Vice-Marshal: 'In case I'm wanted at the Colonial Office, I'll send you a note as often as I change camp. Here below, all I can offer you is moral advice. I eschew power, you see. As every sane man should.' (*Giggles.*) I am no brave man. Focus. Focus. My dragon will . . . which I will best. (*Giggles.*) Are you there? Old Man? Take your seat, Old Man. Take your seat. The concert is about to begin. My nerves are squeaking. Bruce? Are you ready, now? I can – see – see lights. Ahead, a roaring white light. An all-numbing scream is locked within my skull. (*Collapses.*) Its poor body. Its poor, poor body . . .

BRUCE enters.

Are you there?

BRUCE. Yes.

SHAW. Are we ready?

BRUCE. Aye.

SHAW. How many, (*Mumbles.*) Old Man?

BRUCE. Twelve he said.

SHAW (*quietly*). An extra one for luck. An extra one for luck. (*Giggles.*) I'll count each blow to keep my mind, to keep my mind in governance, right? (*Calm.*) Do it. This way I'm me.

We hear a motorbike engine. A white light fills the room.

Scene Fourteen

In M.O.*'s office.* SHAW *and the* M.O. *stand facing each other from opposite sides of a desk. As the* M.O. *sits he flips a metronome into life.*

M.O. Sit down . . . please. Make yourself . . . hmm.

SHAW. Thank you. My relapses – my fevers come very rarely now, sir.

M.O. It's not your malaria. No, no. Which I'm sure you manage very well. But (*Coughs.*) psychological matters. Corporal Inglis (*He looks at a piece of paper.*) . . . he tells me . . .

SHAW. Inglis is a natural psychoanalyst, sir.

M.O. Pardon?

SHAW. He doesn't know it but he is.

M.O. Is he?

SHAW. He doesn't sound like a Freudian – his interventions are a tad brash. But he has a wonderful gift for spontaneity, sir.

M.O. (*smiles*). Very droll.

SHAW. We must not dismiss the lay practitioners too readily.

M.O. Let us set aside Corporal Inglis's observations for a moment. You know of the work of Herr Freud?

SHAW. I ran away, ran away to the army. When I was fifteen. Playing hide-and-seek, I suppose. I lasted two months. They were a crude, bullying lot. I went somewhere where I intended not to be found.

M.O. And did they find you?

SHAW. No. I returned home in mortal shame.

M.O. Did you find what you were looking for?

SHAW. I was trying to be singular but I failed miserably.

M.O. We often return to what we have taken flight from. Herr Freud's work on the interpretation of dreams . . .

SHAW. Scientific Germanism!

M.O. Dreams tell us much about . . .

SHAW. Is this really your area, Doctor?

M.O. I've studied shell shock . . . in the field – war neurosis – related therapies.

SHAW. Erotomaniacs.

M.O. Erotomaniacs? What of em?

SHAW. And pansexualism. The verdict of those who loath the Freudians. As if sex were a rotten apple.

M.O. Psychoanalysis can free people from the past. The war's residue is millions of nightmares.

SHAW. I have overheard in the tea rooms the ladies tell of their latest dreams, in the fond hope of some audacious interpreter discovering in them all sorts of fashionable abominations. They eat their dreams in public, nibbling away at their pathetic secrets like petit fours. I'm afraid this stuff won't wash on me. My personality won't be brought to heel. It does what it wants. And I tag along.

M.O. What of your family?

SHAW. My mother? My mother suffers from religious mania. She lost two sons in the war so she has given herself to China. As a missionary, you understand. She and I did not see eye to eye. As a child I was unamenable. According to her lights. So she beat me and she beat me.

M.O. How . . .

SHAW. With a cane.

M.O. . . . did you respond to the beatings?

SHAW. I built an impregnable tower. I always felt she was laying siege to me. Cartouches and brass rubbings saved me. I'm sure you know all about family inquisitions. Strange how we humans fit together the jigsaw of our emotions.

M.O. Your father?

SHAW. He was naturally lord-like . . . Oh yes, a hard rider and very hard drinker.

M.O. Is that so?

SHAW. No. No, he wasn't anything heroic. He was very diffident. It's no good. (*He stops the metronome.*) I prefer the ambiguities of art, of fiction, to explain how my emotions work. There's a bit in Jeremiah. The Bible.

M.O. An epic choice.

SHAW (*shakes his head*). Not really. It's about a camel. I know camels. I was in Syria for a time. He tells of a wild she-camel used to the wilderness. How's it go? – 'She snuffeth up the wind at her pleasure; in her occasion who can turn her away? All they that seek her will not weary themselves; in her month they will find her.' That's me. As much of me as I can fathom. A bit dirty. A bit wind-blown. (*Giggles.*) Well, aren't we all nowadays soiled goods? Sir.

M.O. I'm sure you would benefit greatly from the method didactic analysis.

SHAW. It's the itch for good and bad together with me, sir.

M.O. I'm going to recommend a London colleague.

SHAW. No thank you, sir.

M.O. At least open yourself to the possibility.

SHAW. I don't find . . . loss worth dwelling on, since it isn't alleviated by knowledge or answers because there are none. We are storytelling animals – that's all. And we write our stories only to find the book is already written. It's the blank white pages that interest me now. The more one knows the more blank pages there seem to be. Empty pages no longer frighten me. May I go now, sir?

M.O. You may. Shaw, you know it is not given to everyone to live out their fantasy as completely as you.

SHAW. It is the price I have extracted for certain services rendered. Loyal services rendered, sir.

M.O. It is a dangerous path to go down. You deliberately muddle fact and fiction.

SHAW. I prefer scandal as a procedure to any scientific method. There you have it.

M.O. I know what you're about.

SHAW. Do you?

M.O. Your idea of the ranks as a self-cure could destroy you.

SHAW. Yes, shock therapy is always risky.

M.O. Shaw. Lawrence. Whatever your name is.

SHAW. This time it's Shaw, definitely Shaw.

M.O. I'm going to recommend you're discharged. Honourable, of course.

SHAW. You needn't trouble yourself, sir. Honourable or otherwise. Not on my account. Sir.

He salutes. M.O. *returns the salute.*

Will there be anything else, sir?

M.O. No. Return to your duties. Dismissed.

SHAW *exits. The* M.O. *goes to a shelf and picks out a Bible.*

Jeremiah . . . Jeremiah . . . (*Finds and reads.*) 'He that humbleth himself shall be exalted.' He that humbleth himself wants to be exalted. Huh. (*He smacks the book shut.*) Bloody foreigner.

SHAW *stands alone outside the door of the* M.O.'s *office.*

SHAW. I am a daydreamer of such long practice. It is somewhat weird to see, step forth in actuality, from through the froth of dream motives, a man . . . a real person with knuckles and spit and to wrestle, exchanging blows, and wonder . . . what am I doing fighting this creature? Where has he come from? Men dream to practise a private insanity safely. My dreams are exhibitions all men can see.

BRUCE *enters.*

John Bruce. I was just thinking of you. Fancy an outing?

BRUCE. No thanks.

SHAW. I'm biking the Brough into town. You can visit the tea shop – I've got some business with the post office. A package to collect.

BRUCE. I'm going across to see the C.O.

SHAW. Are you indeed? (*Long pause.*)

BRUCE. Are you not interested in why?

SHAW. Sorry – why? Why are you going to see the C.O.?

BRUCE. I'm chucking it . . . I'm getting out.

SHAW. It will be a formality. You haven't finished basic yet. Be a little slovenly.

BRUCE. Slovenly?

SHAW. Yes, put on an attitude.

BRUCE. I look alright?

SHAW. Disrespect will speed up the process – the quicker you'll win your freedom.

BRUCE. I want you to know it has nothing to do wi you.

SHAW. What?

BRUCE. My decision to quit.

SHAW. It's tough life, the military. You'll miss the regular routine.

BRUCE. I doubt it.

SHAW. The being cared for, the rails of conduct. A man needs, sometimes, rules and regulations.

BRUCE. To kick against or to bow down in front of? I'm no lie-a-bed. It's just no in me to be jumping through hoops at every turn.

SHAW. In military the person is at a discount. That's the way it is.

BRUCE. Too many folk wi hoops round here. Grease balls I'd put intae next week if they geed me their lip on civvy street.

SHAW. Tolerance of harshness, that's the proof of discipline. Obey the last order given and you can't go wrong. That's my advice.

BRUCE. I'm not cut out for it.

SHAW. I may be on my way myself soon.

BRUCE. Yeah?

SHAW. I'm thinking of the R.A.F.

BRUCE. I wanted to talk to you about . . .

SHAW. The aeroplane, that's the future. The monthly retainer still stands – if you still want it.

BRUCE. Well, yeah.

SHAW. Good.

BRUCE. I want to talk to you about that.

SHAW. There are some tasks I need done on the outside. Hush, hush. Take a job in a given locality. Keep an eye on things.

BRUCE. Just like before?

SHAW. Exactly like before.

BRUCE. Done. (*Goes to shake hands.* SHAW *backs off.*)

SHAW. Must fly.

BRUCE. We'll talk later.

SHAW. Catch you in the canteen. (*Exits.*)

BRUCE. I'll let you know how I get on . . . If you're interested.

Scene Fifteen

The hut before morning kit-inspection. INGLIS *is drinking.* RUDE *is finishing off the last parts of his kit lay-out.* BRUCE *lies on his bed, indifferent.* SHAW *and* UXBRIDGE *are wrestling in mock style.* SHAW *breaks off and puts on the gramophone. We hear: 'Onward Christian Soldiers'.*

UXBRIDGE. He's a slippery bastard.

SHAW. It goes, don't you think, with Inglis and kit-inspection? Ambient.

RUDE. Like chalk an . . . chalk.

INGLIS (*from his room*). Get that thing off! (*Drains his mug.*) This ain't no fuckin church revival. I won't have it.

UXBRIDGE. Like it, Shaw. Suits him to a T. It's your signature tune, Corp. What you complaining about? (*Quietly.*) You stupid pisspot.

SHAW. It's a serious dedication, Uxbridge. I'm not pulling anyone's leg. He is a corporal of the heavenly host.

UXBRIDGE. With bed socks knitted by his old mum in his fucking kit bag . . .

RUDE. . . . and mints to suck when the going gets fucking heavy.

SHAW. A mist of banners and sawing trombones – marching past the Cenotaph.

UXBRIDGE. God bless our veterans.

SHAW. Pure music-hall.

UXBRIDGE (*referring to* INGLIS). Here, he an incense swinger? You know, the hocus-pocus rosary-bead brigade?

BRUCE. He's Protestant. They don't do incense.

UXBRIDGE. No.

BRUCE. You just get yer lug-drum bashed.

RUDE. You'll miss the hut, Jock – you will?

BRUCE. I don't think so.

UXBRIDGE. He'll be drunk tonight, won't you, Jock?

BRUCE. I'll be fu. Blootered, stoochied, oxtered hame. Hammered.

UXBRIDGE. You jocks got more names for drink than Londoners have for ten-bob note.

BRUCE. More than that – more than Eskimos have for snow.

SHAW. I've never been besotted. (*Takes up a book.*)

BRUCE. In a couple of hours I'm gonny saunter out that gate. Catch the slowest mode of transport going. Jump off and on. Stroll about the arcade. Take it nice an slow. Looking forward to tomorrow morning – when I won't be doing parade.

RUDE. Got passing out parade in two days – you could have stayed till then, Jock.

UXBRIDGE. You dipstick.

INGLIS *enters with a clipboard.*

INGLIS. Stand by your beds. Attention. Bruce, you urny oot till noon. On your feet.

BRUCE *gets up, slovenly.*

This is lovely. Not trying to mock, are we? Wrings ma heart, the Sally Ann. This hut gone all religious, has it? Well, has it?

UXBRIDGE. It's the temperance message, Corp.

INGLIS. The temperance message, aye, what about it? (*Turns it off.*)

UXBRIDGE. We've all signed the pledge. Didn't we, lads?

RUDE. We all signed.

INGLIS. You canny write ya dafty. (*Picks up his journal.*) You seen his book, it's full o doodles.

SHAW. It's simply we've all seen what drink can do to a decent chap, Corporal.

UXBRIDGE. It's a tune we think suits the grave and high-minded sense of duty what you have installed in us fighting men.

RUDE. It's gen, Corporal.

SHAW. When we go by the other huts they always stop and pointing, say: 'There go Inglis's holy warriors.'

BRUCE. A finer body o sober loons nae man ever saw.

INGLIS. That so. I'm rarely this impressed with hut banter. I stand back in amazement. And what would your signature tune be, Uxbridge?

UXBRIDGE. I don't know.

INGLIS. I do wonder. Maybe 'Let's Have a Tiddley in the Fountain'.

UXBRIDGE. How's about, how's about Miss Nellie Wallace singing: 'My mother said / Always look under the bed / Before you blow the candle out / See if there's a man about / Always look under the bed.'

RUDE joins in. INGLIS throws a hay-maker but UXBRIDGE ducks and INGLIS barely manages to save himself from falling over.

INGLIS. What are you smirking at? Shaw, what you laughing at?

SHAW. Few things are more comical than the fresh air swipe, Corporal. I'm sure you will concur.

INGLIS. Comical, eh? Comical. Well, we'll just have to see what comical jobs we have on the menu today. Spud-peeling suit you, Shaw? Hmm? That suit you?

SHAW (*steps forward and snaps to attention*). Thank you, Corporal.

INGLIS. Rude, you can join him.

RUDE. Why me, Corp?

INGLIS punches RUDE in the stomach.

INGLIS. If anyone's interested. Uxbridge will be doing funny voices down the toilet block. He will be doing imitations of Lloyd George and extracts from his speeches down the fuckin lavy pan. That merriment enough for you? Those karzies will shine. Know why they'll shine? Cos you will be there licking till fuckin midnight, you French letter. What are you, Uxbridge?

UXBRIDGE. A French letter, Corp.

INGLIS. Now get on that fuckin square.

They all march out. BRUCE *leaves slowly.*

Bruce – a word wi you.

BRUCE. I'm not one for finishing lectures, Corp.

INGLIS. You're easily led, Bruce.

BRUCE. Spare me it, please.

INGLIS. Shaw's got a fuckin ring through your hooter, laddie.

BRUCE. You don't want me late for parade, do you, Corp?

INGLIS. You're not going on parade. You're straight to stores get yer civvy kit. I don't want someone who can't hack it on that square.

BRUCE. Well . . . ta much.

INGLIS. Someone who shirks . . . a sluggard. Someone sneers at sacrifice. Good men.

BRUCE. Fuck your tanks.

INGLIS. What did you say?

BRUCE. You got fuckin cotton wool buds in your lugs? I said fuck your tanks. Fuck your army. Fuck the lot o yous.

INGLIS. I think you deserve a good leathering for that. (*Taking his belt off.*) I think you fuckin young cubs need tae see.

BRUCE. See if you lay a glove on me. I'm warning you.

INGLIS. Call it your passing-out lesson. One that's long overdue. You asked for it, laddie. Flabby civvies posing as soldiers.

BRUCE. I'm fuckin warning you.

INGLIS. Keep the noise down, son, keep it doon. We don't want to be disturbed.

Punches BRUCE, *kicks him, then rains blows from the belt onto him.* BRUCE *reaches his bed-block.*

You fuckin civvy. No trying to run away, are we? We're no finished yet.

BRUCE *pulls out a revolver.*

BRUCE. You bastard. I'll blow your head off.

INGLIS. Fuck sake, laddie. Hold on. Bruce. Put that doon.

BRUCE. God help me I will.

INGLIS. Take it easy. Put that away.

BRUCE. You army fucker.

INGLIS (*crumbles*). Don't point that at me.

BRUCE. I'll blow your head off. Get on yer fuckin knees.

INGLIS. Please don't point it. Please. (*He's on his knees.*) Don't shoot me. Don't shoot me.

BRUCE. Look at the state o you.

INGLIS. Please don't shoot.

BRUCE. Get off. My mither's brothers were in France, Inglis. My Uncle Fraser got home on leave. I can't remember what he looked like. I can't remember any of their faces. I remember playing with his kit, buckles and that.

INGLIS. Don't shoot. Don't shoot.

BRUCE. He came home for a bit of leave. He seemed his jolly old self. Only smoked a lot more, to keep his lungs clear. Morning he was due to go back, Mum found him in bed. Give him his breakfast in bed as a wee treat. He was wearing his gas mask. Sitting there in bed wi the gas mask on. Only thing was, he had a tube from the gas lamp stuck in it. She wouldny let me in but I could hear it hissing. Outside on the landing I could hear . . . hissing.

INGLIS. Don't shoot.

BRUCE. You think they'll chisel his name somewhere, on a nice piece o Kinraddie granite? Shouldny think so. He ran away, didn't he? On your feet. On your fuckin feet! Now, why don't you drop yer breeks . . . Drop yer fuckin trousers.

INGLIS *complies.* BRUCE *goes to leave . . . turns and looks at* INGLIS. *He places the pistol on the table.*

Here. Maybe you can find a use for this . . . Corporal. Plug a hole in your miserable life. (*Exit.*)

INGLIS. Great number of Boche.

Gets up and goes to the pistol. Snatches it up. More shelling noises. Sticks it in his mouth. Can't do it. He's shaking in shock.

Great numbers of Boche. I hivnny got any scars. Great numbers of Boche.

In rage, scatters the kit on UXBRIDGE*'s bed. Goes to* SHAW*'s. Doesn't know what to do. Where to start. Unzips himself and urinates over the bed. Lights fade.*

Great numbers of Boche. Backs to the wall. Great numbers o Boche. Nae scars. Wit do we do?

Crumple of shells.

Scene Sixteen

UXBRIDGE *enters, carrying a mop over his shoulder, looks around. Lights a fag. A metal dustbin is close by, he opens it and retrieves a bottle of ale. Takes a swig. Sees someone coming and quickly replaces the ale bottle.* BRUCE *enters in civvies, carrying a small suitcase.*

UXBRIDGE. It's you. You're a different man in normal togs, Jock.

BRUCE. I feel different.

UXBRIDGE. Yeah?

BRUCE. I am different.

UXBRIDGE. You even stand different.

BRUCE. I'm a civvy – it feels the way it should be.

UXBRIDGE. Good on you. You know. It's flashed through the camp.

BRUCE. What has?

UXBRIDGE. What you think? You're a sly one, Jock. We should have rumbled. He does get undreamed-of odds and ends not even a sergeant gets. He takes his coal from the C.O.'s bucket. Who would believe it? Our billet will be cushy from now on.

BRUCE. That a reason for you staying on?

UXBRIDGE. A right officers' mess.

BRUCE. He cares nothing for frills.

UXBRIDGE. I'm putting in for a stripe, I am. Don't you fret. I'll look out for him. Be his best friend. I'll make a point of it.

BRUCE. His friend? I don't think your ready for that. Friendship wi him is different.

UXBRIDGE. How?

BRUCE. It alters yi. You won't see through him, Uxbridge. His masterpiece is people.

UXBRIDGE. I can admire that in a man, I can.

BRUCE. I judge you can.

UXBRIDGE. He's a proper Houdini, only he don't escape cos he doesn't want to. You should stick around. I'll have him princing about like a wee doggie shortly.

BRUCE. You think so?

UXBRIDGE. I know he looks on us as fucking natives. Well, he's one himself now. A wog.

BRUCE. You're a fuckin wretch, Uxbridge. See you.

UXBRIDGE (*ports arms with the mop*). Attention. Open the gates. Guards, port arms. Hey, Bruce?

BRUCE. What?

UXBRIDGE. Doesn't quite have the same ring to it – does it? Shaw of Dorset. Shaw of Bovington . . . ha-ha.

BRUCE *exits.* UXBRIDGE *plays different rifle drill with his mop.*

He's got dignity, Bruce. He has. Well, maybe not dignity. But he's got the charm. Shaw's got the charm hanging about him all right. The way he draws people to him, villains an all, a right magnet for the tragic fucked-up and the disgraced of name. Like me, Jock. A different kind of grandness hangs about his neck. Takes a crook to smell it. Nothing sticks to him, no power can hold him but he slips through its fingers. You don't see that,

Bruce. You can't. But I do. I do. Fucking wretches do. (*Giggles like* SHAW.)

Scene Seventeen

SHAW *and* RUDE *are peeling potatoes, throwing them into huge bins. A mountain of spuds.*

RUDE. Got a lot to get through.

SHAW. We'll get through them.

RUDE. By dinner time – I doubt it.

SHAW. Just focus.

RUDE. Mountain of them. Jesus Christ, my hands are nipped frozen. I can't go on.

SHAW. Yes you can. It only hurts if you allow it. All you have to do is bear the pain.

RUDE. Can I? Can I?

SHAW. Just empty your head. Come on, I'll race you.

RUDE. No fear. You can't be beat . . . If I get through these, you can show me . . . show me your scars.

SHAW. Yes. As a treat, eh?

RUDE. Yeah, as a treat. You got a lot, Shaw. Just looking at them makes me wince. That one runs round your back is a fuckin monster.

SHAW. Yes, it is.

RUDE. You get that out east?

SHAW. In Arabia.

RUDE. Must've been hellish.

SHAW. No. I'll tell you about the Wadi Rum one day.

RUDE. Was he good for a laugh – a decent bloke, then?

SHAW. Mister Wadi Rum was an excellent chap. Yes.

RUDE. Arabs is funny.

SHAW. To my mind all our subject provinces are not worth one dead Englishman. Of course it's young men like you, Rude, who do the killing.

RUDE. Yeah.

SHAW. Young men whose murderous dispatching mints a new world.

RUDE. Yeah . . .

SHAW. But then the old men come along and it's old men who shape the peace.

RUDE. They think they know everything.

SHAW. Old men with their secret deals. I have seen what the abattoir politics of Empire looks like.

RUDE. What would you say should be my approach, Shaw, if I end up out there – which is likely after all, since we own bleeding half of it? I don't want to offend. Step on anybody's toes.

SHAW. For Arabs the main bugbear with Westerners is the hat.

RUDE (*stops peeling*). The hat?

SHAW. Hats.

RUDE. You mean like your bowler?

SHAW. The hamburg, boater, bowler . . . the lot.

RUDE. Bleeding hell. That's a savage trait, is it not? What's hats got to do with the price of fish?

SHAW. They have a malignant prejudice against the hat and believe our persistence in wearing it is founded on some immoral or irreligious principle. Wear a hat, Rude, and your best Arab friend will be ashamed of you in public.

RUDE. I'll remember that.

SHAW. When you can handle the point of view of another race, Rude, you have become a civilised human being.

RUDE. Thanks for the tip. When in Cairo, go bare-nappered. (*They continue to peel.*) What do you miss most about civvy street? What most?

SHAW. Fruit. I miss fruit.

RUDE. Fruit? You got your apples in the canteen. What else?

SHAW. They gave me the keys to Jesus College. Library. I miss the library. Books. Silly things. Rubbings. Wall climbing. Mock heroic stuff.

RUDE. I miss the farm.

SHAW. You miss the farm? Horse odours and the like?

RUDE. My dad was turfed out. He got farmer's lung. Harvest dust got in his bleeding chest. Invalid he is. What about your pop?

SHAW. The epidemic seen him off. 1919.

RUDE. We moved to Aldershot – soldier town. Me mum loves to be loved so I had plenty uncles. All in khaki.

SHAW. The necessary supply of heroes must be maintained.

RUDE. Spot on. Mustard. Very sharp.

SHAW. Ha! Mustard indeed.

RUDE. I miss dark on the farm. The half-thawed snow outdoors. The bit under blankets just afore cockcrow splits the pitch-black and you hear the milkers throwing about for their boots. (*Points upstairs with his thumb.*) And you lace up your own, hoping there's a nice fire on below. Least ways that's how I opt to recall it.

SHAW. Recall is silly, Rude.

RUDE. No. Why?

SHAW. Because the past is dead.

RUDE. I bet the old place is choked to the rafters wi weeds.

SHAW. The past . . .

RUDE. We used to shoot weasels . . .

SHAW. . . . even as it's remembered, isn't alive.

RUDE. . . . hang them in the woods.

SHAW. There's no rain falls there can soak, no fire in the sun. The pain there has no sting. Nothing hurts at all. It pains to think. Now it pains to think this saying goodbye will not hurt soon. Tomorrow there will be . . . nothing.

RUDE. What goodbye? You mean Jock?

SHAW. Don't you think it should hurt . . . even a little? Somewhat disappointing that it doesn't.

RUDE. You've got us. Uxbridge and me.

SHAW. You're my mates now.

RUDE. We're your muckers. We'll look after you.

SHAW. Yes. We'll all be candid together, eh?

RUDE. Hut F12.

SHAW. There's some things you need to know. It could be dangerous.

RUDE. What's chancy?

SHAW. It could be dangerous, Rude.

RUDE. What do we care?

SHAW. No. I jest not. It involves the Russians.

RUDE. Yeah?

SHAW. Yes. Shhhh.

RUDE. Let them hear.

SHAW. Come here. The eye of Moscow is everywhere.

RUDE (*whispers*). Those Bolsheviks are queer. Corp hates them. Something to do with Ypres or something.

SHAW. Ypres or something?

RUDE. Yes. When the Bolshies gave up. Hun sent twenty divisions west.

SHAW. I understand.

RUDE. Got the shit kicked out them. Backs to the wall. He's got no pals left. Can I ask you something? I've been set on asking you for the longest. But. Phew. Your views means a lot to me. Like being a man of the world an all.

SHAW. Ask away, Sid.

RUDE. Do you . . . do you think I've got . . . got it in me to be a soldier? I means a real soldier.

SHAW. I think you'll make an excellent soldier.

RUDE. First rate?

SHAW. First class.

RUDE. It's what I've always wanted.

SHAW. Yes . . . Mother wants you smart and clean and upright.

RUDE. My mum what?

SHAW. Your mum will be very proud.

RUDE. You looking forward to passing-out parade? She's coming over for it. Who's coming over for you?

SHAW. I sent out no invitations.

RUDE. You got lots of pals.

SHAW. Never be afraid of being shunned, Rude. It's one's shield and shining sword.

RUDE (*holding his bayonet*). Yeah, a shining blade. You like being a soldier?

SHAW. Yes. Very much.

RUDE. Attention. On your feet, trooper. Attention!

SHAW *snaps to attention.*

Stand easy.

SHAW *stands easy.*

Name and number to the officer!

SHAW. T.E. Shaw. T.E. Shaw. 78756, sir. Reporting for duty, sir.

RUDE. You like being a soldier, Shaw? Answer the officer. Answer him at once.

SHAW. It is a gift, sir.

RUDE. A gift? What the fuck you on about, a gift? You here for some mental rest? Mental rest? That it?

SHAW. There is a very rare gift, sir, a man can make.

RUDE. Answer the officer at once.

SHAW. Call it a sacrifice which cancels pride. But few pleasures are this rich.

RUDE. What's the meaning of this, Shaw?

SHAW. This uniform . . . these killing clothes which wall its wearer from ordinary . . . make me a willing victim . . . a contract man sold to the state, my will assigned. And to the peace-loving we are lower than convicts.

RUDE (*mimicking* INGLIS). You're scum, laddie. Fix bayonets. Stab,

1, 2, 3. Stab, 1, 2, 3.

SHAW. Some wear it for the glamour of a military life in Empire but only those . . . only those receive full satisfaction who degrade themselves in unsulking service. A perfect soldier's bond is to be a hired piece on the chessboard of the King . . . A perfect soldier is a handful of dead leaves. Will-less. And as in all perfections there is a hidden selfishness. Very well concealed. (*He smiles.*) T.E. Shaw. 78756, sir. Reporting for duty, sir.

RUDE (*nearly dark onstage*). Attention.

SHAW *complies.*

Stand easy.

SHAW *complies.*

Attention.

SHAW *complies.*

Stand easy.

SHAW *complies.*

Attention.

SHAW *complies. Sounds of warfare. Cinematic images flood over* SHAW.

End.

A Nick Hern Book

The Doll Tower first published in Great Britain as a paperback original
in 2005 by Nick Hern Books Limited, 14 Larden Road, London W3 7ST
in association with LLT, Liverpool's New Writing Theatre

The Doll Tower copyright © 2005 Ronan O'Donnell

Ronan O'Donnell has asserted his right to be identified as
the author of this work

Cover image: Andy Pettener

Typeset by Country Setting, Kingsdown, Kent CT14 8ES
Printed Great Britain by Cox and Wyman Limited, Reading, Berks

A CIP catalogue record for this book is available from
the British Library

ISBN-13   978 1 85459 891 2
ISBN-10   1 85459 891 0